Readings in Literary Criticism 19

CRITICS ON WALLACE STEVENS

Readings in Literary Criticism

CRITICS ON WALLACE STEVENS

Readings in Literary Criticism
Edited by Peter L. McNamara

 University of Miami Press
Coral Gables, Florida

74 - 5925

CONTENTS

ACKNOWLEDGMENTS

Harold C. Ackerman, Jr.: from *Concerning Poetry*, vol. 2, no. 1, Spring 1969. Copyright © 1969 by Western Washington State College. Reprinted by permission of the publisher.

James Baird: from *Studies in Honor of John C. Hodges and Alwin Thayer.* Copyright © 1961 by The University of Tennessee Press. Reprinted by permission of the publisher.

William W. Bevis: from *English Literary History*, vol. 37, 1970. Copyright © 1970 by The Johns Hopkins Press. Reprinted by permission of the publisher.

Frank Doggett: from *ELH: A Journal of English History*, vol. 25, 1958. Copyright © 1958 by The Johns Hopkins Press. Reprinted by permission of the publisher.

Edward Guerschi: from *The Centennial Review of Arts and Sciences*, vol. 8, 1964. Copyright © 1964 by *The Centennial Review.* Reprinted by permission of the publisher.

J. Dennis Huston: from *Modern Philology*, vol. 67, 1970. Copyright © 1970 by The University of Chicago Press. Reprinted by permission of the publisher.

George Lensing: from *Essays in Honor of Esmond Linworth Marilla.* Copyright © 1970 by Louisiana State University Press. Reprinted by permission of the publisher.

George McFadden: from *Modern Language Quarterly*, vol. 23, 1962. Copyright © 1962 by the University of Washington Press. Reprinted by permission of the publisher.

Peter L. McNamara: from *College English*, vol. 25, 1964. Copyright © by the National Council of Teachers of English. Reprinted by permission of the National Council of Teachers of English.

Samuel French Morse: from *Boston University Studies in English*, vol. 2, 1956. Copyright © 1956 by the Trustees of Boston University. Reprinted by the permission of the trustees.

Marjorie Perloff: from *American Literature*, vol. 36, 1964. Copyright © 1964 by Duke University Press. Reprinted by permission of the publisher.

Donald Sheehan: from *Papers on Language and Literature*, vol. 2, 1966. Copyright © 1966 by the Board of Trustees of Southern Illinois University. Reprinted by permission of the trustees.

Wallace Stevens: from *The Necessary Angel.* Copyright © 1951 by Alfred A. Knopf. Reprinted by permission of Random House.

Wallace Stevens: from *Opus Posthumous.* Copyright © 1957 by Alfred A. Knopf. Reprinted by permission of Random House.

INTRODUCTION

THE GREAT "poem" about Wallace Stevens—the central philosophy of his poetry—is yet to be composed, if it can be. Yet the conviction behind this gathering of notes toward that central philosophy is that recent criticism, particularly of the last ten years, is a truer guide to Stevens' poetry than what went before. If there is one pervasive theme implicit in these critiques it is that this poet of paradox, ambivalence, and uncertainty frequently qualifies but seldom asserts. Thus the writers shy from arguing an unvarying poetic creed, consistent patterns of imagery, or simplistic elegance of intent; each individual poem exhibits Stevens' vitality at one stage of a process of constant re-orientation, defining only for that moment "what will suffice." At the same time they eschew the charge of "dandyism" which invalidates much earlier criticism.

Since it is true, as Stevens remarks, that "we never see the world except the moment after," criticism gropes toward perceptions which were gone before the artist made his record, seeks communion with the ashes of experience. Yet this communion has value when the record is the product of acute perception, for in the ashes of the act we find embers to rekindle our own sense of the world. These critics help us perceive how we must sift the ashes of Stevens' experience. George Lensing, for example, turns us to his letters as a ground over which to rove for the fuel of his creativity. William Bevis indicates how the making of *Harmonium* became an irresistible opportunity to poke up the fire by rearrangement. James Baird, Samuel French Morse, and Donald Sheehan uncover the sparks of inspiration while Edward Guereschi, J. Dennis Huston, and Frank Doggett, among others, reflect on the relation between the kindling spirit and individual illuminations.

Then there is Stevens on Stevens, "the necessary angel of earth,/ Since, in my sight, you see the earth again." Excerpts from Stevens' prose light the creative way; while much is vexingly obscure or whimsical, the moments of clarity burn brighter than any attempt at criticism. Preparing the reader for the work of the critics, their ultimate value is to provide an entrée to Stevens' act of the mind, the crux of interest and attention.

University of North Carolina, 1971   PETER L. MCNAMARA

TABLE OF IMPORTANT DATES

1879	October 2, Wallace Stevens born at Reading, Pennsylvania.
1897	Stevens enters Harvard; he contributes to the *Harvard Advocate*, eventually serving as its editor.
1901	Unsuccessful in newspaper work, Stevens enters New York Law School.
1904	June, Stevens enters law practice in New York.
1909	September 21, Stevens marries Elsie Viola Moll (Kachel)
1914	November, Stevens' earliest mature poetry ("Phases," I-IV: *OP*, 3-5) printed by Harriet Monroe in *Poetry*.
1916	March, Stevens joins New York office of Hartford Accident and Indemnity Company. May, Stevens transfers to Hartford as director of a subsidiary of Hartford Accident.
1923	September 7, Alfred Knopf publishes *Harmonium*, Stevens' first collected volume. Marianne Moore gave it a favorable reception in her review for *The Dial* (January 1924).
1934	Stevens named Vice-President, Hartford Accident and Indemnity Company.
1935	*Ideas of Order* (Alcestis Press).
1936	*Owl's Clover* (Alcestis Press).
1937	*The Man with the Blue Guitar* (Alfred Knopf).
1942	September, *Parts of a World* (Alfred Knopf).
1947	*Transport to Summer* (Alfred Knopf).
1950	Stevens receives the Bollingen Prize in Poetry of the Yale University Library (for 1949).
	The Auroras of Autumn (Alfred Knopf).
1951	*The Necessary Angel*, Stevens' prose studies of artistic theory (Alfred Knopf).
1954	October 1, *The Collected Poems* published on Stevens' seventy-fifth birthday. Alfred Knopf had overcome Stevens' objections to the collection (*L*, 829) and vetoed Stevens' proposed title, *The Whole of Harmonium* (*L*, 834).
1955	Stevens awarded the Pulitzer Prize and National Book Award. August 2, Stevens succumbs to cancer.
1957	*Opus Posthumous* (Alfred Knopf).
1966	*Letters of Wallace Stevens*, edited by Holly Stevens (Alfred Knopf).

STEVENS ON POETRY

THE IMAGINATION loses vitality as it ceases to adhere to what is real. When it adheres to the unreal and intensifies what is unreal, while its first effect may be extraordinary, that effect is the maximum effect that it will ever have.

(NA, 6)

The subject-matter of poetry is not that "collection of solid, static objects extended in space" but the life that is lived in the scene that it composes; and so reality is not that external scene but the life that is lived in it.

(NA, 25)

The poetic process is psychologically an escapist process. The chatter about escapism is, to my way of thinking, merely common cant. My own remarks about resisting or evading the pressure of reality mean escapism, if analyzed. Escapism has a pejorative sense, which it cannot be supposed that I include in the sense in which I use the word. The pejorative sense applies where the poet is not attached to reality, where the imagination does not adhere to reality, which, for my part, I regard as fundamental.

(NA, 30-31)

The way a poet feels when he is writing, or after he has written, a poem that completely accomplishes his purpose is evidence of the personal nature of his activity. To describe it by exaggerating it, he shares the transformation, not to say apotheosis, accomplished by the poem.

(NA, 49)

The incredible is not a part of poetic truth. On the contrary, what concerns us in poetry, as in everything else, is the belief of credible people in credible things. It follows that poetic truth is the truth of credible things, not so much that it is actually so, as that it must be so. It is toward that alone that it is possible for the intelligence to move. . . . The incredible is inexhaustible but, fortunately, it is not always the same. We come, in this way, to understand that the moment of exaltation that the poet experiences when he writes a poem that completely accomplishes his purpose, is a moment of victory over the incredible, a moment of purity that does not become any the less pure because, as what was incredible is eliminated, something newly credible takes its place.

(NA, 53)

And having ceased to be metaphysicians, even though we have acquired something from them as from all men, and standing in the radiant and productive atmosphere, and examining first one detail of that world, one particular, and then another, as we find them by chance, and observing many things that seem to be poetry without any intervention on our part, as, for example, the blue sky, and noting, in any case, that the imagination never brings anything into the world but that, on the contrary, like the personality of the poet in the act of creating, it is no more than a process, and desiring with all the power of our desire not to write falsely, do we not begin to think

of the possibility that poetry is only reality, after all, and that poetic truth is
a factual truth, seen, it may be, by those whose range in the perception of
fact—that is, whose sensibility—is greater than our own? From that point of
view, the truth that we experience when we are in agreement with reality is
the truth of fact. In consequence, when men, baffled by philosophic truth, turn
to poetic truth, they return to their starting-point, they return to fact, not, it
ought to be clear, to bare fact (or call it absolute fact), but to fact possibly
beyond their perception in the first instance and outside the normal range of
their sensibility. What we have called elevation and elation on the part of the
poet, which he communicates to the reader, may be not so much elevation as
an incandescence of the intelligence and so more than ever a triumph over the
incredible.

(NA, 59-60)

The poet is constantly concerned with two theories. One relates to the
imagination as a power within him not so much to destroy reality at will as
to put it to his own uses. He comes to feel that his imagination is not wholly
his own but that it may be part of a much larger, much more potent imagination, which it is his affair to try to get at. For this reason, he pushes on and
lives, or tries to live, as Paul Valery did, on the verge of consciousness. This
often results in poetry that is marginal, subliminal. The same theory exists in
relation to prose, to painting and other arts. The second theory relates to the
imagination as a power within him to have such insights into reality as will
make it possible for him to be sufficient as a poet in the very center of
consciousness. This results, or should result, in a central poetry.

(NA, 115)

A poet writes of twilight because he shrinks from noon-day. He writes about
the country because he dislikes the city, and he likes the one and dislikes the
other because of some trait of mind or nerves; that is to say, because of
something in himself that influences his thinking and feeling. So then, the poet
and his subject are inseparable. There are stresses which he invites; there are
stresses which he avoids. There are colors that have the blandest effect on him;
there are others with which he can do nothing but find fault. In music he likes
the strings. But the horns shock him. A flat landscape extending in all
directions to immense distances placates him. But he shrugs his shoulders at
mountains. One young woman seems to be someone that he would like to
know; another seems to be someone that he must know without fail.

(NA, 122)

The imagination is one of the great human powers. The romantic belittles
it. The imagination is the liberty of the mind. The romantic is a failure to make
use of that liberty. It is to the imagination what sentimentality is to feeling.
It is a failure of the imagination precisely as sentimentality is a failure of feeling.
The imagination is the only genius. It is intrepid and eager and the extreme
of its achievement lies in abstraction. The achievement of the romantic, on the
contrary, lies in minor wish-fulfillments and it is incapable of abstraction.

(NA, 138-39)

The truth seems to be that we live in concepts of the imagination before the reason has established them. If this is true, then reason is simply the methodizer of the imagination. It may be that the imagination is a miracle of logic and that its exquisite divinations are calculations beyond analysis, as the conclusions of the reason are calculations wholly within analysis. If so, one understands perfectly the remark that "in the service of love and imagination nothing can be too lavish, too sublime or too festive." In the statement that we live in concepts of the imagination before the reason has established them, the word "concepts" means concepts of normality. Further, the statement that the imagination is the power that enables us to perceive the normal in the abnormal is a form of repetition of this statement. One statement does not demonstrate the other. The two statements together imply that the instantaneous disclosures of living are disclosures of the normal.

(NA, 154)

The paramount relation between poetry and painting today, between modern man and modern art is simply this: that in an age in which disbelief is so profoundly prevalent or, if not disbelief, indifference to questions of belief, poetry and painting, and the arts in general, are, in their measure, a compensation for what has been lost.

(NA, 170-71)

Our own time, and by this I mean the last two or three generations, including our own, can be summed up in a way that brings into unity an immense number of details by saying of it that it is a time in which the search for the supreme truth has been a search in reality or through reality or even a search for some supremely acceptable fiction.

(NA, 173)

According to the traditional views of sensory perception, we do not see the world immediately but only as the result of a process of seeing and after the completion of that process, that is to say, we never see the world except the moment after. Thus we are constantly observing the past. Here is an idea, not the result of poetic thinking and entirely without poetic intention, which instantly changes the face of the world. Its effect is that of an almost inappreciable change of which, nevertheless, we remain acutely conscious. The material world, for all the assurances of the eye, has become immaterial. It has become an image in the mind. The solid earth disappears and the whole atmosphere is subtilized not by the arrival of some venerable beam of light from an almost hypothetical star but by a breach of reality. What we see is not an external world but an image of it and hence an internal world.

(OP, 190-91)

The habit of forming concepts is a habit of the mind by which it probes for an integration. Where we see the results of that habit in the works of philosophers we may think that it is a habit which they share with no one else. This is untrue. The habit of probing for an integration seems to be part of the general will to order. We must, therefore, go a step farther and look for the respect that separates the poet and the philosopher in the kind of integrations for which they search. The philosopher searches for an integration for its own sake, as, for example, Plato's idea that knowledge is recollection or that the soul is a harmony; the poet searches for an integration that shall be not so much sufficient in itself as sufficient for some quality that it possesses, such as its insight, its evocative power or its appearance in the eye of the imagination. The philosopher intends his integration to be fateful; the poet intends his to be effective.

(*OP*, 196-97)

It remains true, however, that the probing of the philosopher is deliberate. On the other hand, the probing of the poet is fortuitous. I am speaking of the time before he has found his subject, because, once he has found his subject, that is to say, once he has achieved the integration for which he has been probing he becomes as deliberate, in his own way, as the philosopher. Up to the point at which he has found his subject, the state of vague receptivity in which he goes about resembles one part of something that is dependent on another part, which he is not quite able to specify.

(*OP*, 197)

One is always writing about two things at the same time in poetry and it is this that produces the tension characteristic of poetry. One is the true subject and the other is the poetry of the subject. The difficulty of sticking to the true subject, when it is the poetry of the subject that is paramount in one's mind, need only be mentioned to be understood. In a poet who makes the true subject paramount and who merely embellishes it, the subject is constant and the development orderly.

(*OP*, 221)

Ordinarily the poet is associated with the word, not with the act; and ordinarily the word collects its strength from the imagination or, with its aid, from reality. The poet finds that as between these two sources: the imagination and reality, the imagination is false, whatever else may be said of it, and reality is true; and being concerned that poetry should be a thing of vital and virile importance, he commits himself to reality, which then becomes his inescapable and ever-present difficulty and inamorata. In any event, he has lost nothing; for the imagination, while it might have led him to purities beyond definition, never yet progressed except by particulars. Having gained the world, the imaginative remains available to him in respect to all the particulars of the world. Instead of having lost anything, he has gained a sense of direction and a certainty of understanding. He has strengthened himself to resist the bogus. He has become like a man who can see what he wants to see and touch what he wants to touch. In all his poems with all their enchantments for the poet himself, there is the final enchantment that they are true. The significance of the poetic act then is that it is evidence. It is instance and illustration. It is an illumination of a surface, the movement of a self in the rock. Above all it is a new engagement with life. It is that miracle to which the true faith of the poet attaches itself.

(*OP*, 240-41)

From *The Necessary Angel* (New York: Knopf, 1951) and *Opus Posthumous* (New York: Knopf, 1957).

JAMES BAIRD

Transvaluation in Stevens' Poetics

THE MODERNITY of Wallace Stevens is here regarded as the focus upon which contemporary criticism should first direct its attention. Mr. Howard Nemerov has recently spoken of the poetry of Stevens as "the difficult art of a man who, so far as thought is concerned, may prove to have been the only truly *modern* poet of his time."[1] If there is difficulty in this poetry, a difficulty of a kind encountered by all serious percipience of modern expression in the arts, then a reading of Stevens must begin with the first problems. The inquiry must be philosophical; we must seek to know what it is in the poetic craft of this artist which distinguishes him as modern. Lest there appear to be a suggestion here that the problem is marked by the vulgar circumstance of art wrought merely as originality or obscurity, it should be said at once that Stevens, as a projector of a life of feeling rooted in our century, could have been only what he was. His poetry is none other than the record of a man's sense of *being,* of what it is to be as one's self in an age which is very largely stripped of tradition and myth. Stevens himself has left us the radical question. "What is the poet's subject? It is his sense of the world."[2] He regarded the life of feeling as wholly individual, and informing of this sense. "The truth is that a man's sense of the world dictates his subjects to him and that this sense is derived from his personality, his temperament, over which he has little control and possibly none, except superficially. It is not a literary problem. It is the problem of his mind and nerves."[3]

This study deals with the distinction of a first problem in our reading of Stevens and suggests a critical means of resolving it. The great contribution of Stevens to modern art is found in his transvaluation in poetics, his record of a major shift in the direction of poetic theory. Quite possibly, the highest assertion of Stevens's poetry, "Notes Toward a Supreme Fiction," will take its place among the landmarks of poetic theory. These landmarks of recent origin may be taken as dominant records of transvaluation: Wordsworth's *The Prelude* (version 1805) in its analysis of the imaginative process in poetic genesis; *Biographia Literaria* of Coleridge with its theory of poetic synthesis; Poe's concept of poetic unity and impressionistic totality; Baudelaire's *l'Art romantique* with its doctrine of the poetic symbol as a structure of polyvalence; the essays of Mallarmé which establish a ground for poetic surrealism, and the related forms of cubist and abstract painting. Within such originations as these we discover the directions which have brought us to the thresholds of modern poetry; and it is in this succession that the "supreme fiction" of Wallace

14   JAMES BAIRD

Stevens assumes a contemporary authority. His transvaluation is a crossing into what may seem to many of us a bleak domain for poetry. Though we may choose to leave the question of its universality to a later generation, nonetheless it is a modern domain which we survey.

Stevens had admitted to one universality, and only one, in the realm of contemporary poetry. His description of this reality in the valedictory piece called "The Rock" has not been regarded as of his best writing. But we must attempt to understand it as he accepted it, if we would trace the poetic architecture which he fashioned, from first verse to last, with a beautiful and meticulous consistency. The rock is the gray ledge of being. It is obdurate, cold, and uninteresting until the imagination clothes it with bright leaves. It is merely existence, shall we say, like the hard mineral being of any rock substance of the universe. To this comes the poet, the man of imagination. "The poem makes meanings of the rock, / Of such mixed motion and such imagery / That its barrenness becomes a thousand things / And so exists no more." Standing in this man's presence, we ask: what continues; what makes tradition; what, belief? He answers: the rock and the imagination continue, nothing else. The solitariness of the individual bears upon us relentlessly in "Notes Toward a Supreme Fiction": "From this the poem springs: that we live in a place / That is not our own and, much more, not ourselves / And hard it is in spite of blazoned days." There is only the bare fact of existence, an existence stripped of myth and philosophy. Yet one bright possession remains, the green vitality of the imagining man; and by this, modern man, as Stevens saw him, must assert his courage and endure his predicament.

That this artist has left us a poetry of "philosophical color," comparable to the philosophical color of Wordsworth in *The Prelude,* or to that of Paul Valéry in *La Jeune Parque,*[4] for instance, we can immediately agree. Yet to read him as a dialectician is to ignore his avowed dismissal of philosophy, and to forget that he was a poet passionately desirous of being understood, so much so that he wished to give us explication in the very act of creation. There is a perseverance of transvaluation throughout the poetic career of Stevens. The total range of his lyricism is a poet's record of the attainment of his poetics, his plotting of the ground upon which he builds, with few presuppositions and postulates. Thus we have that unusual combination—it would seem one almost without precedent—of the reach toward theory, in and through the very moment in which the object is rendered poetically, and of the description in which the poet rests as the imagination shapes a form. This is precisely the combination evident in the familiar "Sea Surface Full of Clouds," where the sea is shaped in accordance with the commands of the poet's sovereign imagination, a sea changing in color from moment to moment, but arrested periodically in its metamorphosis as a poetics is formulated: the imagination, the poet says, is doing this: *C'était mon enfant, mon bijou, mon âme.*

What appears to be dialectic, in the sense of relationship to philosophical method, is but the sign of an intense search for a new poetics, as in the compelling necessity expressed in these lines from "Things of August":

> The meanings are our own—
> It is a text we shall be needing . . .
> A text of intelligent men
> At the centre of the unintelligible,
> As in a hermitage, for us to think,
> Writing and reading the rigid inscription.

These are the acts of modern man, modern man the poet, as Stevens sees him: living at the center of the unintelligible, he places his meanings upon the gray rock of reality; he lives in his own hermitage; he writes his own inscription upon the rock, and then he reads it to himself. Philosophical color in Stevens was inevitable, for it is precisely this color which must make the rock endurable. The poet has become a demonstrator of possibilities for endurance rather than the spinner of myth or the mirror of a universal faith.

If we then begin with a recognition of transvaluation in the poetics of Stevens, there appear to be certain ways open to us for an understanding of its character. Four of these will be suggested here as critical approaches. The first appears in our encounter with what Stevens has called *modern reality*. Speaking at the Museum of Modern Art in New York in 1951 on the relations between poetry and painting, Stevens observed: "Modern reality is a reality of decreation, in which our revelations are not the revelations of belief, but the precious portents of our own powers." The greatest truth is that "man's truth is the final resolution of everything."[5] The position taken by this poet becomes, then, clearly existential. Experience does not pass through transmutation into essence and absolute. The world is shattered, and then reordered by the imagining man, the poet. In this vision of "decreation" appear two succeeding approaches: Stevens's close affinity to recent French poetics, and his relation to modern painting, especially to that of French cubism and early non-objectivism. A fourth is concomitant to the first, in Stevens's assumption that modern reality, in his sense, displaces every inherited absolute. It may be clearly traced in his evaluation of American impoverishment in myth and faith.

I

"We live in a place / That is not our own," Stevens contends in his supreme fiction, that fiction which is poetry, and in no sense universal truth. Paul Tillich, in a recent essay on the existentialism of contemporary painting, discovers through modern art the central fact of our being-now: "Mankind does not feel at home in this world any more." He continues: "The categories have lost their embracing and overwhelming and asserting power."[6] We do not assume a justification of Stevens's poetics through contemporary theology. But it is pertinent to note certain analogies between Tillich's existentialism, here intent upon a reading of modern painting, and the existential position which Stevens maintains in his concept of modern reality. Once again we hear him on the relations between poetry and painting in our century. "The world about us would be desolate except for the world within us. . . . The arts in general, are, in their measure, a compensation for what has been lost. Men feel that the imagination is the next greatest power to faith: the reigning prince. Consequently their interest in the imagination and its world is to be regarded not as a phase of humanism but as a vital self-assertion in a world in which nothing but the self remains, if that remains."[7] Neither *Weisheit* nor *rabbi*, as Stevens symbolizes philosophy and the builder of ideal systems in his poetry, has any place here. With an awesome acceptance Stevens says to us in "Notes Toward a Supreme Fiction": "I have not but I am and as I am, I am." This means: I have only selfhood; I am as of the now, as I am. One adds to this the imagination as the expression of selfhood. It builds the world. The dismissal of philosophy agrees with the existentialist's view expressed by Tillich: if we would understand existentialism, we must look at modern art; there is more in this looking than in reading modern philosophy.[8] The achievement of Wallace Stevens in poetry is supremely explicative of this modern evidence. It springs from a commitment at the exact center of his poetics. Here he speaks again in an address on the imagination and "its power to possess the moment it perceives": "Like light, it adds nothing, except itself. . . . It colors, increases, brings to a beginning and an end, invents language, crushes men and, for that matter, gods in its hands. . . . "[9]

Both Tillich and Stevens speak here in the existential mode. Every essentialism is rejected. Modern art, without myth and without tradition, forms in the hands of each creator the shape of his being-now, encompassed as this is with the individual's sense of his alienation from every system and every proposition which formerly generated that human power called belief. It has been suggested that contemporary phenomenology will serve us in our approach to Stevens.[10] So it would seem. Jean-Paul Sartre, for instance, will illuminate Stevens when he says: "The [imaginative] intention is at the center of consciousness; it is [this] intention that envisages the object, that is, which makes it what it is. . . . The object as an image is therefore contemporaneous with the consciousness I take of it, and it is determined exactly by that consciousness. . ."[11] The phenomenon of the object in consciousness rests in what Sartre calls, existentially, "quasi-observation." The object as image is never anything more than the consciousness one has of it.[12] With all this Stevens as theorist is in agreement. We are not concerned with this proximity between two modern thinkers as a matter of influence. It is, simply, that both men speak with the voice of modernity.

Thus, in "Things of August," Stevens names the poverty in which we must begin to make constructions of this world. Each of us is born empty-handed, an artisan without tools in the barrenness around us.

> The world images for the beholder.
> He is born the blank mechanic of the mountains,
>
> The blank frere of fields, their matin laborer.
> He is the possessed of sense not the possessor.

> He does not change the sea from crumpled tinfoil
> To chromatic crawler. But it is changed.

A man does not change the reality of sea; yet it becomes for him successively foil or machine, or a thousand things. He casts his colors upon the rock of being, on which all objects appear ephemerally through imagination, and disappear. Philosophy is false happiness, the idea that by thinking one can synthesize appearances, and make a truth. For the end of philosophy is bleakness. It lies, the poet says, "A foyer of the spirit in a landscape / Of the mind, in which we sit / And wear humanity's bleak crown" ("Crude Foyer").

II

The true antecedence of the poetics of Stevens is French, an antecedence which begins in the Parnassians and the *symbolistes*. The significance of symbolic polyvalence in Baudelaire's theory and practice and that of the floating image in the poetry of Rimbaud are clearly in the swift movement of poetry toward its present. Yet these significant French expressions are not in themselves the major points of departure which one follows toward Stevens. It is better first to acknowledge the "French climate" in which this American poet flourishes. For evidence, one needs at hand a certain token knowledge of this modern Gallic state of poetry as it appears throughout the range of Wallace Stevens: his frequent references to French theorists in his addresses, his particular fondness for the French title and the French phrase in his poetry, and his impressive knowledge of French painting from Poussin to Braque, Picasso, and Villon. He is aware of that "liberation of poetry to mere chance" which was first manifested in Mallarmé's rejection of syntactic relationships; and he understands the transition from Mallarmé into painting (*e.g.,* the cubism of Marcel Duchamp). His knowledge of the rise of modernism in the art of France is usually wide and astute. The testament of this knowledge appears in the fibre of the poetry; and it has yet to be fully exposed.

The tokens of agreement are impressive for the critic of Stevens. In *l'Art romantique* Baudelaire had regarded the whole of the visible universe as a store of images. It is the imagination of the poet which gives these images place and value. Without his act, they are unrelated, and meaningless. Thus, Baudelaire establishes the conditions of theory which make the full existentialism of Paul Valéry, to whom Stevens refers in his discussions of poetry as *act*. With Valéry, to construct a poem is to construct the self. "The poetic art has as its counterpart an art of self-fulfillment by means of the acts which beget the poem, an art of overcoming 'that familiar chaos' (*i.e.,* the disorder of psychological life), of conferring a form, a style, upon that which 'lacks it by nature . . . ' "[13] In the sense of Valéry nature must be regarded as the familiar chaos of perception and emotion, of external and phenomenal experience and of that human internality of a fluid world of ideas. Nearly the earliest of Stevens's poetry grasps this concept of an art which gives shape to nature. The now famous text of "The Idea of Order at Key West" is closer to Paul Valéry than to any poet of Stevens's native background. The voice of the girl symbolizes the voice of the poet. She sings beside the "grinding water and the gasping wind." She sings "beyond the genius of the sea"; "She was the single artificer of the world / In which she sang." "Then we, / As we beheld her striding there alone, / Knew that there never was a world for her / Except the one she sang and, singing, made." To the frequently advanced contention that this singer is very much like Wordsworth's Highland lass of "The Solitary Reaper," it must be said that a solitary singing girl is the only point of resemblance, a resemblance, at that, which does not go beyond the surfaces of the poems. Nature is not given order and form by the song of a girl in Wordsworth's lyric. Nature is absolute, and the song is merely a signal for a series of associations, widening as concentric circles do about a stone cast into water. Stevens points away from rather than toward his inheritance in English poetry.

Beyond this affinity with Valéry lie the wider possibilities of Stevens as related to the early French surrealists. "Under each stone," wrote Tristan Tzara, "there is a nest of words, and it is out of their rapid whirling that the substance of the word is formed."[14] In the view of Marcel Raymond, Tzara became through this doctrine the founder of a school of poets who, more consciously than ever before in France, "identified the problem of poetry with the crucial problem of existence."[15] Stevens in America is wholly companionable. For what is his lyric, "The Glass of Water," other than a poet's evidence of a nest of words uncovered beneath a familiar object? The glass stands before us. "Light is the lion that comes down to drink." The commonplace, the stern reality, the water in the glass, becomes a tropic pool. Water weeds appear, and in the new green depths, "the plastic parts of poems crash in the mind." The analogies are equally impressive when one compares Stevens with Guillaume Apollinaire, in the poem "Zone," for instance, where the poet contends that the heritage of romanticism and symbolism is dead weight. We have no choice, in the ambience of Apollinaire's poem, but to accept a world of Now. There is no antiquity, no myth to support us; for poetry, he says, we have only a "loudly singing poster," and for prose only a newspaper and a dime novel.

III

We perhaps already agree that Stevens is the most versatile colorist in contemporary poetry in English. We have long since recognized the brilliant palette of *Harmonium;* and we know his use of primary colors as symbols for the poet's faculties: blue for the imagination objectively considered, red for high sensuousness, green for vitality, that energy which often seems to mark the poet's youth, as in the Florida pieces, with the teeming vigor of a jungle. We understand, too, that Stevens takes from Juan Gris and from Picasso the image of the guitar, rendered again and again in the cubist painting of these masters, and that he uses it as his symbol of the poet's song. As a symbolic device, the instrument appears in "Of Modern Poetry," in "Jouga," in "Notes

Toward a Supreme Fiction," in "The Auroras of Autumn," and in other pieces. But these are all poetic devices within technique. The important concern is with Stevens's poetics in relation to the aesthetics of modern painting.

Leo Stein, whom Stevens quotes in his lecture on poetry and painting, has written of contemporary art: "In the pictorial one sees as though the pictured thing were seen within the limits of a frame, which marks the plane to which the focus is referred."[16] The imposition of the frame upon the object presented, as though to limit it from other objects and endow it with the particular consciousness which one brings to it, is exactly to limit the act of the imagination to a given present. We must hold strictly here to modern painting in its existential character, and dismiss for the present the meaning of the frame in Renaissance painting, for instance, where the mythological or religious picture is, rather, a token of an infinite series. In modern art the object is claimed within bounds. Even when it displays metamorphosis, as in "Landscape at Céret" by Juan Gris, it is nonetheless framed. The reference is to one moment in an artist's perception of a landscape, to an absolute infinity of the landscape presented. Framed, the object is only what it is to the individual painter *imagining*, as of now.

Paul Tillich has said that most modern art has transformed all reality into forms of still life. The transformation requires our critical understanding. "It means that organic forms have disappeared, and with them has disappeared idealism which is always connected with the description of organic forms. The forms of our existence are not more organic. They are atomistic, disrupted. These disrupted forms of our existence are taken by themselves by modern artists as the real elements of reality. . . . "[17] Tillich, as theologian, is, of course, concerned with ontology. The forms of our existence are shattered. Therefore, the painter works with "the original elements of reality which in the physical realm are cubes, planes, colors, lines, and shadows."[18] The limits of the frame within which the focus is placed, as seen by Leo Stein and by Tillich, are equivalent.

This agreement is important because it strengthens our understanding of this modern principle from painting as Stevens applies it to poetry. Again and again he gives us the still life (*e.g.,* "A Bouquet of Roses in Sunlight"), or adjuncts of it (*e.g.,* "Woman Looking at a Vase of Flowers"). But the study of a shattered reality evident in French cubism is only, for Stevens, the point of departure in these poems. What we are given by Stevens is not concern for what lies in pieces, but rather for what may be brought from the dull gray of the actual world to the color of object consciousness. Reality is framed again and again, but it is forever the reality of the gray rock, made endurable by the color conferred by the imagination. So in "The Bird with the Coppery, Keen Claws" of *Harmonium:* "He munches a dry shell while he exerts / His will, yet never ceases, perfect cock, / To flare, in the sun-pallor of his rock." The bird is the color of the poet's devising. He is the object of the imagination conferred, in all his splendor, upon reality. This dun bird, munching a dry shell, flares up from the pallor of the rock, touched by the light of a poet's imagining, and by his will. He is framed, related to no other bird. In this time of a man's imagining he flares into poetry in a burnished flame.

The Cubist Painters, that remarkable document of Guillaume. Apollinaire, gives us exactly what Stevens has told us in his poetry. "Without poets, without artists, men would soon weary of nature's monotony. . . . There would be no seasons, no civilization, no thought, no humanity; even life would give way, and the impotent void would reign everywhere."[19] Again: "We do not know all the colors. Each of us invents new ones."[20] In his poem, "The Man on the Dump," Stevens rejects an enslaving monotony of tradition. There must be a purifying change, amid this dump heap of old images. Yet the purity of matter remains, Nature to be acknowledged and colored anew.[21]

> That's the moment when the moon creeps up
> To the bubbling of bassoons. That's the time
> One looks at the elephant colorings of tires.
> Everything is shed; and the moon comes up as the moon
> (All its images are in the dump) and you see
> As a man (not like an image of a man),
> You see the moon rise in the empty sky.

This is the phenomenon of quasi-observation, in the sense of Sartre. The object becomes other than what it is through consciousness informed by imagination. The sky is washed clean, we may conclude, as a gray slate is washed. It is wholly cleared of centuries of accreting images. There the poet begins anew. It is his own view of evening. Automobile tires are elephant-colored. There is a fresh moonrise to woodwind music. Cynthia and Endymion, Diana, attendant night-ingales, the vigils of pale courtly lovers—a universe of symbols and images and a universe of myth are gone. Nor is this familiar and constantly addressed heavenly body William Butler Yeats's old moon, "crazed through much child-bearing," the symbolic death of imagination among modern men. It is the material moon, issuing a kind of light, merely and quite barely there in the evening sky to become a new reality for a new poet.

IV

It is true that Stevens has given us a myth: the sun he calls "gold flourisher," being "in the difficulty of what it is to be"; its light stirs the imagination; and from this we trace a poet's private legend. But we wish to inquire of his humanity, of what he saw and felt as universal. For his private legend, in all its extensions, is but myth that eulogizes myth. This is true, though he has told us that "what makes the poet the potent figure he is, or was, or ought to be, is that he creates the world to which we turn incessantly. . . ."[22] The first and one of the most impressive of Stevens's poems relating to the loss of myth disavows the possiblity of a new belief for our time: "The Paltry Nude Starts on a Spring Voyage." She is Venus, now weary, scudding the glitter of the sea, noiseless, on one more wave. She is not of Botticelli, we may be sure. She is paltry, wishing for purple stuff upon her arms, as in the richness of some other Renaissance image. Her play is meagre in the scurry of her voyage. Yet, in a later day, she may go seaward again, a nude more golden than ever before. She was legend once, she was belief. What will she be anew? Who is to say?

Between Venus and "The Rock" with its stern acceptance of the one reality lie the years in which Stevens assumed his American identity. The corpse that is carried down the stairs in "Mozart, 1935" is the death of our manly youth, and the dirge is of our present, a dirge of a jazz piano, "its hoo-hoo-hoo, / its shoo-shoo-shoo, its rac-a-nic, / Its envious cachinnation," Mozart was young, and we, we are old. The same corpse has passed in "The Emperor of Ice-Cream," where the roller of big cigars gives us our "concupiscent curds," and love is amorousness in the corner drug store. Venus is there again, under the sheet, cold and dumb. In "The American Sublime" Stevens asks: "How does one stand / To behold the sublime, / To confront the mockers, / The mickey mockers . . . "? Did Mr. Walt Disney, indeed, give us our mythology? In "Dance of the Macabre Mice" we of the "land of turkeys in turkeyweather" go round and round a statue and admire our beautiful history; but the statue is covered with mice. Have we, the Mickey-mockers, found our myth in the mouse, on Thanksgiving Day? Or who is more solitary than the American poet? Here he stands alone. The poet looks down in his imagining from hotel room 2903 in "Loneliness in Jersey City": "The Steeples are empty and so are the people. . . . " The questions rise inevitably from these poems. They express a peculiarly American inquiry of Stevens. Beneath their whimsicality and their irony there lies an illimitable sadness.

Stevens has left us a poetics specifically wrought for our time. In his act of transvaluation he assumes his modern eminence. His words, as he spoke of modern poetry and painting stand for him, and, no doubt, for many of us in this present. These arts, as he thought of them, are sources of our present conception of reality. They are the supports of a kind of life, which seems to be worth the living. But through them living itself becomes "only a stage in the endless study of an existence, which is the heroic subject of all study."[23]

There have been many absolute judgments in the name of poetics. One often feels, on rereading Wordsworth and Coleridge, for instance, that these poets assumed an unchallengeable sovereignty in theory. There is a like conviction in Valéry. Perhaps the final disclosure of Wallace Stevens's modernity appears to us in his calm acceptance of our certain transience. He certainly knew the full nature of the transvaluation in poetics which he projected. Yet he would be the last to say that this regard of the vital function of poetry will endure infinitely. He believed that we have only existence to study. But the imagination which colors existence can in no sense be unchanging. Nor can one presuppose that imagining men will never again live by myth.

The forms of modern art point into change and impermanence. It is this truth for Stevens that informs the most poignant of all his visions, that given us in "A Postcard from the Volcano." Children in another age will pick up our bones, little knowing that once we were "as quick as foxes," and in the autumn of grapes had "a being, breathing frost." Least will they guess that what we left with our bones was "what we felt / At what we saw."

NOTES

1. "The Poetry of Wallace Stevens," *The Sewanee Review,* LXV (1957), 13.
2. "Effects of Analogy," in *The Necessary Angel* (New York, 1951), p. 121. This address was delivered by Stevens as a Bergen lecture at Yale in 1947.
3. *Ibid.,* p. 122.
4. See Marcel Raymond's discussion of Valéry in *From Baudelaire to Surrealism* (New York, 1950), p. 163.
5. *The Necessary Angel,* p. 175.
6. "Existential Aspects of Modern Art," in *Christianity and the Existentialists,* ed. Michalson (New York, 1956), p. 141.
7. *The Necessary Angel,* pp. 169, 171.
8. Tillich, p. 129.
9. *The Necessary Angel,* pp. 61-62.
10. Nemerov, pp. 6-7.
11. *The Psychology of the Imagination* (New York, 1948), p. 13.
12. *Ibid.,* p. 20.
13. Raymond, p. 155.
14. *Ibid.,* pp. 316-17.
15. *Ibid.,* pp. 298-99.
16. *Appreciation: Painting, Poetry, Prose* (New York, 1947), p. 104.
17. Tillich, pp. 136-37.
18. *Ibid.,* p. 139.
19. *The Cubist Painters: Aesthetic Meditations,* tr. Lionel Abel, Documents of Modern Art (New York, 1944), p. 13.
20. *Ibid.,* p. 9.
21. "Notes Toward a Supreme Fiction," Section 1.
22. *The Necessary Angel,* p. 31.
23. *Ibid.,* p. 176.

From *Studies in Honor of John C. Hodges and Alwin Thayer,* ed. Richard B. Davis and John L. Lievsay (Knoxville: Univ. of Tennessee Press, 1961), pp. 163-73.

SAMUEL FRENCH MORSE

Some Ideas About The Thing Itself

ALTHOUGH IT is perfectly clear that for Wallace Stevens "poetry is the subject of the poem," very few readers will be satisfied to let the matter rest easily in such general terms. Until the last few years of his life, Stevens confined his theorizing to demonstrations: that is, he did not separate poetic theory from poetic practice; what he had to say *about* poetry he said in his poems. Like Pope in the *Essay on Criticism,* Stevens preferred making his point concretely, in context, to speculating abstractly about the point. Admittedly, he indulged in a good deal of abstraction in the poems themselves, but always in relation to particulars. The measure of his success must therefore be the persuasiveness of his theory as practice. Such a strategy risks a good deal, but it implies a greater respect for poetry as making, for the thing itself, and for the poet as maker, than most academic poetic theory and much criticism.

Indeed, one of the great difficulties in dealing critically with Stevens has derived from his refusal to separate theory and practice. He has written more poems explicitly "about" poetry than any of his other contemporaries. The title of his second book is *Ideas of Order* (1935); and a simple count of the poems that in their titles mention poetry or some aspect of it makes an awareness of this bias inescapable: "Poetry Is a Destructive Force," "The Poems of Our Climate," "Add This to Rhetoric," "Of Modern Poetry," "Poésie Abrutie," "Thinking of a Relation between the Images of Metaphors," "Men Made Out of Words," "The Motive for Metaphor," "Analysis of a Theme," "The Ultimate Poem Is Abstract," "The Poem That Took the Place of a Mountain," "Long and Sluggish Lines," etc. Stevens' interest in poetic and aesthetic theory, and in "life as it is lived in the imagination" pervades the whole body of his poetry, whatever his titles may be, whatever his apparent subject, whether it be "Sailing after Lunch," "Le Monocle de Mon Oncle," or "An Ordinary Evening in New Haven."

The essays on poetry and the imagination which Stevens gathered together under the title *The Necessary Angel* (1951) cast much light on this concern; but even in his essays Stevens writes more as a poet than as a critic or theorist. The essay "The Realm of Resemblance" is simply one panel of the "Three Academic Pieces," and requires the two "illustrations," the two poems that accompany it, to make its implications clear. The illustrations interact with the essay; each part informs the others. Even though "Three Academic Pieces" can be considered an exception among the essays, Stevens composed his other prose pieces in much the same way. In "The Noble Rider and the Sound of Words," the examples used to illustrate various concepts of nobility become the very substance of the argument the essay develops. Rich, as the essays are, they do not furnish skeleton keys to the poems. They suggest rather than define. What they say has to be understood in the way the poems must be understood. For the most part, the poems have to be worked out in their own terms.

Not that the poems are so difficult as some critics have made them out to be. Furthermore, certain characteristic and constantly recurring devices furnish clues, and fairly broad ones. The poems of *Harmonium* (1923) set the tone of the poetry as a whole: humorous, gay, ironic, almost diffident at times, but self-possessed and always concerned with opposites of one kind or another. "Earthy Anecdote," which stands at the beginning of *Harmonium,* is a case in point. The poem is contrived wholly of oppositions: bucks and firecat, lines right and lines left, bristling and sleep. Similar patterns of oppositions recur again and again. Analogously, many poems compose from a series of alternatives or variations. Thus Crispin, the hero of "The Comedian as the Letter C," goes through a series of adventures, from change to change, rather than to a fixed and final dogma. His conclusion amounts to nothing more than an ultimate acceptance of his limitations; but as a character, he is more than the sum of his parts, and his adventures are shaped by his character, just as his character shapes his adventures. Crispin begins by asserting that "man is the intelligence of his soil"; but after voyaging to America and undergoing a series of disturbing and unsettling experiences, he comes to think that "his soil is man's intelligence." This, however, is not his final conclusion. Having discovered "how much / Of what he saw he never saw at all," he must reconcile these opposite assertions. He does so by accepting both assertions; or at least he does not reject absolutely the one in favor of the other. Crispin has come to know the world well enough not to take it solemnly. Having come to accept his limitations, which are synonymous with the limitations of his own sensibility and his own experience, he makes the best of them by enjoying life. He settles down to a cabin and a family. Although his relation to the universe has been "clipped," his imagination makes up for what his life and outward experience lack. Thus he is free to let his imagination range to *its* limits.

The most surprising thing about this poem is its point of view. The reader sees Crispin from a perspective larger than that from which Crispin sees himself, but at the same time obliquely through Crispin's own eyes, as in indirect discourse—that is, with a certain amount of intimate detachment. Stevens makes Crispin both an illustration and an embodiment of the ideas that his hero lives by. Unless one gets the right perspective on Crispin, however, the poem dissolves into a bewildering concatenation of images and sounds. What Stevens assumes, I think, is that all words spoken in his poetry are spoken not in his own private person but in his capacity as poet. Although critics have complained about the weakness of the dramatic impulse in Stevens' work, very few have noticed that a large number of the poems are written from the point of view of a character, usually a character making an aside or meditating, interpreting, as if to himself. The "I" of such poems, like the "one" or "he" or "she" of others, is undoubtedly often very close to Stevens himself, but there can be no exact equation of person and poet. No poem by a writer of such great detachment is likely to be purely autobiographical.

In the later poems, the identity of the intelligence that composes these "notes toward a supreme fiction" becomes elusive. Even so, if one has caught the perspective from which the poems of *Harmonium* become visible, the later work gives up a good many of its secrets quite willingly. Oppositions continue to be posed, alternatives stated, variations played. The poems become more and more like astonishingly skillful improvisations, like the bagatelles into which Beethoven poured so much of his most extraordinary inventiveness and insight during his final years. In these later poems the possible combinations of oppositions, alternatives, variation, and improvisation multiply enormously, both in form and substance, insofar as one can separate the two for purposes of discussion here. They never really separate in practice, of course, as the Canon Aspirin in "Notes toward a Supreme Fiction" comes to realize:

> He had to choose. But it was not a choice
> Between excluding things. It was not a choice
>
> Between, but of. He chose to include the things
> That in each other are included, the whole,
> The complicate, the amassing harmony.

An even more characteristic example is "Connoisseur of Chaos," from *Parts of a World* (1942), which employs all Stevens' manners and modes in a way that would have delighted Pope in their resolution of apparently contradictory elements. Like Pope, Stevens has a sense of a universal order that art "discovers" rather than "devises." The relevant passage from Pope is the "key" passage from the *Essay on Criticism,* which comes fairly early in Part I, beginning with "First follow *Nature* . . . " and concluding with:

> Those *Rules* of old discover'd, not devis'd
> Are Nature still, but Nature methodiz'd;
> Nature, like Liberty, is but restrain'd
> By the same Laws which first herself ordain'd.

After making the necessary allowances for historical differences, certain real resemblances remain. It is possible to think of Pope as no more than a moral essayist who wrote in verse, but to do so is to separate his form from his matter. Pope's ideas as poetry are as useful as they ever were, even though the philosophy his poetry was officially supposed to expound is outmoded. What he "means" is essentially what any poet means. Insofar as the *Essay on Criticism* is a poem, it "discovers" rather than "devises" order, as "the pensive man" who is the "connoisseur of chaos" apprehends through the eagle's eye the order of the "intricate Alps."

To read Pope as philosophy is to destroy Pope as a poet. At the same time, it cannot be denied that his poetry has significance analogous at least to that of philosophy. Stevens put his finger on this problem some years ago in his answer to a questionnaire sent him by the editors of the *Partisan Review:*

> It seems that poetic order is potentially as significant as philosophic order. Accordingly, it is natural to project the idea of a theory of poetry that would be pretty much the same thing as a theory of the world based on a coordination of the poetic aspects of the world. Such an idea completely changes the significance of poetry. It does what poetry itself does, that is to say, it leads to a fresh conception of the world.

Just so the *Essay on Criticism* leads to a fresh conception of the Neoclassic tradition.

The resemblances to Pope in Stevens' work do not, incidentally, stop here. Echoes of Pope's rhetoric and tone and even prosody abound in "The Comedian as the Letter C" and "Le Monocle de Mon Oncle," and in *Harmonium* as a whole. But the influence persists even in the later poems, as, for example, in "Esthétique du Mal," originally published in 1944, and included in *Transport to Summer* (1947):

> And then that Spaniard of the rose, itself
> Hot-hooded and dark-blooded, rescued the rose
> From nature, each time he saw it, making it
> As he saw it, exist in his own especial eye.
> Can we conceive of him as rescuing less,
> As muffing the mistress for her several maids,
> As foregoing the nakedest passion for barefoot
> Philandering?

First of all, the "rescue" of the rose from nature by the artist reflects the Neoclassic doctrine of the superiority of art over nature. Even more pointed, however, is Stevens' use of a figure from a passage in the *Essay on Criticism* which follows almost immediately the famous "key" passage:

> Then Criticism the Muse's handmaid prov'd
> To dress her charms, and make her more belov'd:
> But following wits from that intention stray'd,
> Wo could not win the mistress, woo'd the maid.

The poet—the artist—discovers the whole, if only momentarily, and will not be satisfied with "less." Finally, not to linger over this point too long, it is instructive to observe Stevens' remarks about surrealism:

> The essential fault of surrealism is that it invents without discovering. To make a clam play an accordion is to invent, not to discover. The observation of the unconscious, so far as it can be observed, should reveal things of which

we have previously been unconscious, not the familiar things of which we have been conscious plus imagination.

Here again Stevens confirms Pope's belief that "discovery" takes precedence over what is "devis'd," and that imagination is superior to fancy.

These fragments of conviction, like almost everything else Stevens wrote, in prose or verse, as critic or poet, are full of suggestions for an accurate reading of his work. In one sense, Stevens is the least evasive or oblique, although one of the purest, of modern poets. Whatever he has to reveal he reveals fully and openly, or as fully and openly as any art grounded in metaphor allows, with tremendous gusto. He puts all his cards on the table, including the significant nonsense of life, which, he says, "pierces us with strange relation." He withholds nothing that the reader needs to know, although, as numerous critics have observed, his vocabulary is frequently rather odd. Even so, one has the dictionary. The fondness for queer words, of which the same critics have made so much, is no affectation; his vocabulary is far less impenetrable than that of some of the critics themselves. For the most part, Stevens uses language with extraordinary precision and particularity, and with enough detachment to save it from becoming purely private. He would never be guilty, as Hart Crane was, of using "panis angelicus" to mean "angelic Pan," nor of using a word without first making sure that it said what it meant and meant what it said. At their best, his inventions and nonsense words are perfectly transparent. Nor should he be accused of inventing the name "Badroulbadour" in "The Worms at Heaven's Gate," for example, when he is referring to Aladdin's wife, so named in the *Arabian Nights*. Stevens was also aware that "Badroulbadour" is Arabic for "moon of moons," as he once took the trouble to point out.

Furthermore, since in poetry the sound of a word is part of its meaning, Stevens is certainly justified in using an expression such as "The squirming facts exceed the squamous mind." The rightness of the sound is inextricable from the preciseness of the statement. The strangeness of the words themselves is not, then, merely decorative, but a means to an end. Taken together, all these elements combine to reveal an attitude which is itself part of the ultimate meaning of the words. The playfulness of the vocabulary gets into the line and into the syntax as well, to the extent of determining the seriousness of the statement as a whole.

It is this kind of multiplicity of vision and thought that makes criticism of Stevens so difficult. Even when he appears to separate ideas into their component parts, he does not really do so. He divides *Notes toward a Supreme Fiction* into three units of ten sections each (plus a dedicatory stanza and an epilogue): "It Must Be Abstract," "It Must Change," and "It Must Give Pleasure." The actual effect of the poem is not one of progression so much as of expansion, what he calls in a later poem, "endless elaboration." At the same time, *Notes toward a Supreme Fiction* does have coherence: something very much like the devices of alternation, variation, opposition, and improvisation, employed with enormous skill, serves to balance and control the expansion.

Analogously, one poem suggests another as contrast and complement.

"Owl's Clover" (first published in a limited edition in 1936, and in a revised and considerably cut version, in 1937, in *The Man with the Blue Guitar*) is really a complement of "The Comedian as the Letter C." "An Ordinary Evening in New Haven" (in *The Auroras of Autumn,* 1950) is the complement of *Notes toward a Supreme Fiction* (first published in 1942). The poems do not compete with each other, nor do they cancel each other out. Each is the confirmation of the other. Stevens himself observed that often one poem suggested another, and that he liked to see one poem set in relation to another, although the poems had no obvious or immediate connections. Many of his longer poems composed of several sections can be broken up into self-contained parts, although the cumulative effect of reading them as wholes is vastly rewarding.

Read with the kind of attention that they deserve, the poems make such observations almost superfluous. Yet the passage from "Esthétique du Mal" cited earlier involves another aspect of Stevens' work that has caused considerable confusion. More often than not, Stevens could have said, modifying the cliché with the astuteness of an expert lawyer, "The characters in the following pages are entirely fictitious, and any resemblance to actual persons, dead or alive, is only that basic resemblance wherein 'in some sense, all things resemble each other.'" It is not necessary to know who the actual Spaniard of the rose is in "Esthétique du Mal." Stevens tells the reader all that he needs to know in order to understand what Stevens is showing him. The Spaniard is the artist, the poet, the maker. Knowing that he is Pedro Dot, the rose hybridizer of Barcelona, is of no importance poetically speaking. What matters is that the Spaniard is explicitly, rather than symbolically, a maker. Tracking down originals in Stevens is a little like studying the paintings of Renoir in terms of the identity of the models who posed for them. Again and again Stevens answered inquiries about characters or references in his work by pointing out that he had no specific actual person in mind, but that by accident he hit upon the name of a real person. Stevens created his characters to have their being in the poems; they have significant existence within the poem, not because they have counterparts in "real" life. Their "real" life is the life they possess in the poems, and this is true even though the reader knows that Santayana, for example, is the philosopher in "To an Old Philosopher in Rome."

One cannot stretch the poem to accommodate the actual person without distorting both person and poem. Stevens is no more given to trivial and perverse disguises in the matter of names than he is in his vocabulary. He was not afraid of actual persons or places whenever he wanted to use them: Dufy, Pascagoula, Mozart, Brahms, Whitman, Bossuet, Jersey City, Moscow, Segovia, Marx. Generally, too, he meant the person and the place he named, not something else. His symbolism, whenever it appears in the poems, is essentially a natural symbolism.

As a poet, then, Stevens is a comedian, and his poetry belongs to the tradition of comedy. Theories of comedy are notoriously inadequate, if only because the motives for laughter and reconciliation run the gamut of human experience. The thing itself—comedy or reality or poetry—is always larger than the most commodious definition one can frame for it. Stevens knew this well enough;

his poetry is concerned with the idea from beginning to end. Starting from the premise that the whole is greater than the sum of its parts, and believing that the whole is large enough to include and reconcile all apparently irreconcilable opposites, Stevens is free to demonstrate not only that the real and the imagined are aspects of the same thing but also that they may be one and the same.

Finally, the seriousness of his poetry must be reckoned against his conviction that "poetry is one of the sanctions of life." It is not life; it is not the only sanction of life. But it may be, and it is, for Stevens, the best evidence that life is worth living, as he puts it toward the end of *Notes toward a Supreme Fiction:*

> An occupation, an exercise, a work,
>
> A thing final in itself and, therefore, good:
> One of the vast repetitions final in
> Themselves and, therefore, good, the going round
>
> And round and round, the merely going round,
> Until merely going round is a final good . . . .

"The pleasures of merely circulating" become an affirmation of great significance; they are the visible evidence of life itself.

As early as 1915, in "Peter Quince at the Clavier," Stevens observed that

> Beauty is momentary in the mind—
> The fitful tracing of a portal;
> But in the flesh it is immortal.

His poems are "beauty in the flesh," "a few things for themselves," his testament of the value of life. Knowing this, one knows how to look at a poem such as "The Poem That Took the Place of a Mountain," written sometime in 1952:

> There it was, word for word,
> The poem that took the place of a mountain.
>
> He breathed its oxygen,
> Even when the book lay turned in the dust of his table.
>
> It reminded him how he had needed
> A place to go in his own direction,
>
> How he had recomposed the pines,
> Shifted the rocks and picked his way among clouds,
>
> For the outlook that would be right,
> Where he would be complete in an unexplained completion:

The exact rock where his inexactnesses
Would discover, at last, the view toward which they had edged,

Where he could lie and, gazing down at the sea,
Recognize his unique and solitary home.

Both the poem and the mountain become visible in a single stroke; the vision of the one is the vision of the other, and each achieves its own identity by what can only be called "the secretions of insight."

Rather than charging Stevens with an inability to "think" or "understand" things, it would be more just to say that Stevens knew the intellect was not enough, certainly not enough for a poet. Poetry is something more than an intellectual construct; and the mind is more than intellect. It is the astonishing vitality of Stevens, regardless of his intellectual profundity or lack of it, that makes him so much a poet we cannot do without. He restores to poetry one of its most valuable qualities: the power to shape the world to its own ends.

From *Boston University Studies in English,* 2 (1956), 55-64.

DONALD SHEEHAN

Stevens' Theory of Metaphor

PERHAPS THE most surprising aspect of the criticism of Wallace Stevens is the curious agreement that Stevens is on some counts confused or unclear—especially concerning such basic concepts as "metaphor" and "reality." In dealing with a poet who for so long elaborated two or three ideas, one would be wise to consider where the confusion lies: in the poet or in his critics. Anyone reading Stevens' views on metaphor quickly discovers their intimate relation to his views on reality—and here the trouble begins. Stevens' poetic world is split by an unresolved dualism concerning the nature of reality. Sometimes reality can be "a thing seen by the mind, / Not that which is, but that which is apprehended" (CP, 468) by the poet's metaphors. At other times direct contact with reality can be avoided by metaphors, by "the intricate evasions of as" (CP, 468). That Stevens makes no direct attempt to resolve the dualism is taken as evidence of his supposed confusion.

Yet such an approach seems to me wholly wrong. Though Stevens quite clearly states that

> Over and over again you have said,
> This great world, it divides itself in two, (CP, 218)

he is not by any means lost in a hopeless muddle. Stevens did not consider the dualism destructive; in fact he saw it as necessary to his view of the world. Though he never evolves a tightly ordered theory of metaphor, he does hold to a consistent point of view. And it is this view he constantly elaborates.

"The accuracy of accurate letters is an accuracy with respect to the structure of reality" (NA, 71). With this semiserious preciseness, Stevens begins the first part of "Three Academic Pieces," his only sustained prose discussion of metaphor. The discussion turns on the idea of resemblance. To construct a theory of poetry, Stevens says, requires an examination of the structure of reality. And the resemblance between things is "one of the significant components of the structure of reality" (NA, 71). In nature, Stevens continues, "all things resemble each other," as, for example, the sky and its reflection in the sea resemble one another (NA, 71). "So, too, sufficiently generalized, each man resembles all other men, each woman resembles all other women, this year resembles last year. The beginning of time will, no doubt, resemble the end of time" (NA, 71-72). This resemblance constitutes a relation, a bond between things. Similarly, in metaphor things resemble one another—but with greater fluidity and range than in nature, since, "in metaphor, the resemblance may be, first, between two or more parts of reality; second, between something real and something imagined . . . ; and, third, between two imagined things . . . " (NA, 72). Thus the structure of metaphor resembles the structure of reality.

Yet, as Stevens quickly notes, "We are not dealing with identity" (NA, 72). Stevens does not, as one critic holds, posit "the fluidity of essence,"[1] a world in which one thing is the same as another. For Stevens such a world would be a surrealistic nightmare where a clam plays an accordion. The metaphor or the resemblance does change reality by adding perceived resemblances to it (and so Stevens suggests metamorphosis might be a better word), but it does not abandon, transcend, or totally transform reality. If as Northrop Frye has stated, the "theoretical postulate of Stevens' poetry is a world of total metaphor, where the poet's vision may be identified with anything it visualizes,"[2] then resemblance would vanish and both nature and poetry become purely mechanical. And as Stevens says (NA, 73),

> Nature is not mechanical to that extent for all its mornings and evenings, for all its inhabitants of China or India or Russia, for all its waves, or its leaves, or its hands. Its prodigy is not identity by resemblance and its universe of reproduction is not an assembly line but an incessant creation. Because this is so in nature, it is so in metaphor.

"Nor are we," Stevens goes on, "dealing with imitation" (NA, 73). Though admitting the distinction between imitation and resemblance to be a nicety, Stevens describes imitation as an "identity manqué," something "artificial" and "not fortuitous as a true metaphor is" (NA, 73). Though imitation may imitate something in nature and thereby "escape the derogatory," it often imitates something in metaphor and is thereby lifeless, "and that, finally, is what is wrong with it" (NA, 73).

After dismissing these two aspects, Stevens deals with resemblance itself. The essential attitude throughout Part I of "Three Academic Pieces" is one of caution; Stevens constantly pulls back from absolute statements. This attitude is irritating to the literary theorist, for Stevens simply will not define precisely what metaphor means to him. Instead, much as he does in the poems, he presents aspects, parts of a world, refusing to deal with first causes (or "theoretical postulates") or ultimate ends (theoretical knowledge). Yet Stevens clearly does *imply* the existence of such absolutes—if only to establish where he does not wish to go. It is crucial, though, to see clearly what Stevens is *not* doing, to see what poles he will approach but not embrace.

---

1. Sister M. Bernetta Quinn, O.S.F., "Metamorphosis in Wallace Stevens," reprinted in *Wallace Stevens: A Collection of Critical Essays*, ed. Marie Borroff (Englewood Cliffs, N.J., 1963), p. 63.
2. Northrop Frye, "The Realistic Oriole: A Study of Wallace Stevens," *Fables of Identity* (New York, 1963), p. 251.

One pole is similar to Frye's world of total metaphor—poems such as "Extracts from Addresses to the Academy of Fine Ideas" (*CP*, 252) and "Chocorua to Its Neighbor" (*CP*, 296) approach this absolute pole. Derived ultimately from German epistemology, this pole conceives knowledge as the coalescence of subject (perceiver) and object (perceived). This coalescence, neither wholly subject nor wholly object, but both together, is reality. In this reality, in this "third world" created from the union of the perceiver's and the perceived's, being and knowing are identical; that is, existence and knowledge of existence are the same. In Stevens' poems this reality, as Stevens says elsewhere, created by metaphor, makes the original reality of the perceived thing seem unreal (*OP*, 169). In such poems appear the vague outlines of a myth of the "central man," as Stevens calls him, "Who . . . sums us up." Yet the myth is never articulated, never fully constructed, for Stevens' suspicion of its worth is not to be allayed. It is something to toy with since it is obviously a powerful poetic idea—but for Stevens something to leave alone since, after all, "things as they are" (*CP*, 165) are all that there is.

The other pole is the one Stevens, with his Imagist inheritance, stays closest to.[3] This pole conceives reality as a *thing*, "one and immutable, wholly external, and irreducible."[4] In Stevens, this reality is the world of objects existing apart from any perception of them; it is the world of "things as they are" before becoming "things as they seem." This reality is Stevens' *donné;* it is immediate yet in essence mysterious since the objects constituting it have no reference beyond themselves nor any relation to the perceiver. This reality, then, is unknowable—in contrast to the total knowledge of metaphoric reality.

Between these two extremes, reality as metaphor and reality as unknowable thing, Stevens discusses the idea of resemblance. His aim both in the prose and in the poems, is to keep between the extremes since both culminate in silence: the silence of a dream and the silence of a thing. Stevens distrusts the former and refuses to accept the latter. The poet's sensibility, Stevens continues in "Three Academic Pieces," discovers resemblances between various real and imagined things; his poems articulate such discoveries. This is not merely perception—though resemblance begins with perception—since it is not the eye that creates resemblances but the mind. The eye sees; the mind perceives a resemblance between the thing perceived and something else, either real or imagined; and such a resemblance "touches the sense of reality" (*NA*, 77) since something new is revealed about the thing seen, something new is known. The "desire for resemblance is the desire to enjoy reality" (*NA*, 78), therefore, since resemblance reveals "a new knowledge of reality"—"Not Ideas about the

3. For a recent, succinct summation of Stevens' lifelong relation to Imagism see John Enck, *Wallace Stevens: Images and Judgments* (Carbondale, Ill., 1964), chap. 1, especially pp. 7-12. Enck's book (to which I am most indebted) has the virtue of refusing to force Stevens' poetic concepts into a rigid and falsifying precision, allowing instead the poems to assume their rich and flexible complexity.

4. Lionel Trilling, "Reality in America," *The Liberal Imagination* (New York, 1954), p. 18.

Thing but the Thing Itself" (*CP*, 534). It is in this sense that "poetry is a part
of the structure of reality" (*NA*, 81)—that is, poetry is a knowledge of reality's
arrangement—which, Stevens goes on, "pretty much amounts to saying that
the structure of poetry and the structure of reality are one or, in effect, that
poetry and reality are one . . . " (*NA*, 81).

This is the extent of Stevens' prose discussion of metaphor.[5] In one sense,
as Frye holds, Stevens' "conception of metaphor is regrettably unclear"[6] since
it steadily refuses to resolve in any direct way the dualism concerning reality.
Yet such a refusal is not (as Frye and others would have it) intellectual
muddiness but a key to Stevens' real vitality. Stevens' profound distrust of "the
lunatic of one idea / In a world of ideas" (*CP*, 325) is what lies immediately
behind this. Though unwilling to fit his ideas on metaphor into a rigid scheme,
Stevens is quite willing to take "the steps to this particular abstraction"—but
always with the belief that it is "an ascent through illusion which gathers round
us more closely and more thickly . . . the more we try to penetrate it" (*NA*,
81). That attitude forms the basis of Stevens' view.

And the view, though it cannot be schematized, is consistent and coherent.
The basis of it is that material reality, "things as they are," cannot be known
by a fixed view; one must continually shift one's perspective simply because
"things as they are" are themselves in flux: things live and die, the seasons
change, civilizations rise and fall. Yet what interests Stevens are not the
unknowable mutations (Eliot's and Pound's ancient and modern worlds) but,
simply, the immediate world of reality. "I am what is around me" (*CP*, 86) is,
indeed, his only "theory." In this view the dualism concerning reality is
functional, not destructive: sometimes one sees reality as metaphor; at other
times one sees it as unknowable thing. One moves between these extremes.

The poetry symbolizes this movement by the cycle of the seasons. Stevens'
seasons are states of imaginative perception, moving from summer, when
reality is metaphor, to winter, when reality is unknowable thing, with autumn
and spring partaking of both realities. These states are constantly flowing one
into the other, yet paradoxically, maintaining qualitative uniqueness. In the
imagination's summer the world is what you say it is; that is, the word and
the thing are one, and reality *is* the poet's metaphors. In summer "things as
they are" become "things as they seem." It is the fecund time when images
call forth other images, resemblances create resemblances, and the world is
created in its noblest form (*august* as month and as dignity is a favorite pun).
It is the time when the poet's metaphors (his "seemings") approach total reality
in themselves, without reference to "things as they are":

> If seeming is description without place,
> The spirit's universe, then a summer's day,

5. "Effects of Analogy" (*NA*, 107-30), as the title suggests, deals more with the source and effect
of metaphor than with metaphor itself. Yet all the prose, in both *NA* and *OP*, shuns really direct
treatment of the topic—an approach essential to Stevens' view.
6. Frye, p. 247.

> Even the seeming of a summer's day,
> Is description without place. It is a sense
>
> To which we refer experience . . . . (*CP*, 343)

It is a time when "There is nothing more inscribed nor thought nor felt" (*CP*, 372), since inscription, thought, and feeling are manifestations of strivings, of something still to be attained, still possible. Summer is "arrested peace" and the "Joy of such permanence, right ignorance / Of change still possible" (*CP*, 373). It is a world of metaphor—and, for the moment, complete. Stevens' delight in such a world is profound because this world represents the highest poetic power.

Yet summer contains its own decay since such creation results in "the barrenness / Of the fertile thing that can attain no more" (*CP*, 373). To paraphrase Stevens' title, metaphor is a self-destructive force. When metaphor in itself begins to create a reality totally without reference to things as they are, it then becomes a lifeless abstraction which warps reality. The fertile thing becomes barren and summer goes stale simply because summer fixes the world in its words—and the world will not be fixed. As the connoisseur of chaos says, "A violent order is disorder" (*CP*, 215). Summer becomes quickly the exhausted Appollonian on his mountaintop. Summer is, in the end, only a possibility—

> It is possible that to seem—it is to be (*CP*, 339)

—and as the possibility approaches total actuality, it hardens into nonsense and deception.

Stevens' autumn is the confusion resulting from summer's deceptions. If summer was the momentary coalescence of subject and object, then autumn is the dissolving of the union, the falling away. In autumn the once fertile images of summer distort the changed and changing reality of "things as they are": "The sky is a blue gum streaked with rose. The trees are black"; and summer is seen as a "fat beast," ugly and exhausted, bloated and serene (*CP*, 62). The sky is "a junkshop, / Full of Javelins and old fire-balls, / Triangles and the names of girls" (*CP*, 218)—the trash of an antiquated mythology created by metaphor. Autumn is a time of utter confusion between word and thing—as in "Metamorphosis" (*CP*, 265-66):

> Yillow, yillow, yillow,
> Old worm, my pretty quirk,
> How the wind spells out
> Sep - tem - ber . . . .
>
> Summer is in bones.
> Cock-robin's at Caracas.

> Make o, make o, make o,
> Oto - otu - bre.
>
> And the rude leaves fall.
> The rain falls. The sky
> Falls and lies with the worms.
> The street lamps
>
> Are those that have been hanged,
> Dangling in an illogical
> To and to and fro
> Fro Niz - nil - imbo.

The dilemma here is peculiarly autumn's: summer's vision has been realized (it is "in bones") while reality has changed to autumn: "Cock-robin's at Caracas." The poet attempts to alter his view by "making o"—that is, by seeing things as they are in autumn—yet all he can manage is a nonsensical attempt to merge Caracas' summer with his autumn by verbally clubbing together the Spanish "Octubre" and the English "October." While the leaves and rain of autumn fall, so does summer's sky to lie "with the worms" of summer's imagery. The poet's only vision is of himself—absurdly as a street lamp—"Dangling in an illogical" limbo. Nothing coheres in autumn because coherence is a falsification carried over from summer.

Yet autumn is at the same time an escape from summer's deceptions and sterility. Since in autumn metaphor is deception, images are discarded and reality is faced anew: "One rejects / The trash . . . You see the moon rise in an empty sky" (CP, 202), freed of images about it. "Tired of the old descriptions of the world" (CP, 204), one must learn to exist without any description of existence, to change "From a doctor into an ox" (CP, 204) without knowledge and thus free himself from his words:

> It was how he was free. It was how his freedom came.
> It was being without description, being an ox.
> It was the importance of the trees outdoors,
> The freshness of the oak-leaves, not so much
> That they were oak leaves, as the way they looked.
> It was everything being more real, himself
> At the centre of reality, seeing it.

One then sees the world as an ignorant man sees it, without any ordering, only seeing it. It is in this sense that "One's ignorance is one's chief asset" (OP, 178). And "One feels the purifying change" (CP, 202) as one sees things anew.

As autumn moves into winter one begins (as in summer) to approach a pole: reality as unknowable thing. If autumn is the attempt to see the object as it is, then winter is the consequent silence. The winter world is stripped of all relationships, of all "resemblance," a world in which the object is without reference to anything else or to any observer. It is a bare, chill world of silence when one "Knows desire without any object of desire" (CP, 358), when one's speech is stilled as in sleep:

> He is not here, the old sun,
> As absent as if we were asleep.
>
> The field is frozen. The leaves are dry.
> Bad is final in this light.
>
> In this bleak air the broken stalks
> Have arms without hands. They have trunks
>
> Without legs or, for that, without heads.
> They have heads in which a captive cry
>
> Is merely the moving of a tongue . . . . (CP, 293-94)

Yet this very muteness contains the possibility of summer; as Pack puts it, "the very barreness of winter becomes the source of a new vision."[7] The exhilarating perception in autumn becomes the saving perception in winter— by perceiving things *exactly* as they are one can begin to speak the "new orations of the cold" (CP, 96) out of the perceptions. Such "new orations" speculate upon the possible world of reality as metaphor:

> To discover winter and know it well, to find,
> Not to impose, not to have reasoned at all,
> Out of nothing to have come on major weather,
> It is possible, possible, possible. It must
> Be possible . . . . (CP, 404)

Such speculations upon possibilities are regenerative; they postulate the imagination's existence and power in a world inimical to it. This "fiction of an absolute" (CP, 404), this possiblity of summer's metaphoric reality, is the "crude compoundings" of a "supreme fiction" that will lead to the discovery of reality. Thus, winter, like autumn and summer, is a dualistic world, containing both the imagination's death and its life, its poetic sterility and its poetic potency.

And the rebirth of possibility gives way to the imagination's spring. In spring the imagination makes its first tentative transformations of simple perception into complex resemblance, re-establishing a world of relationships

---

7. Robert Pack, *Wallace Stevens* (New Brunswick, N.J., 1958), p. 141. Pack rightly sees the importance of the seasons but fails to see their ironic nature—that each has its limits—and so does what Stevens will not do: hypothesize a "third world" for poetry (see chap. 3, especially pp. 59-62).

where desire and the object of desire are known and where summer's vision
becomes still more possible:

> There might be in the curling-out of spring
> A purple-leaping element that forth

> Would froth the whole heaven with its seeming-so . . . . (CP, 341)

Yet (as these lines show) Stevens is skeptical of the spring vision; he tends to
see it as slightly insane, too wildly frothing "the whole heaven with its
seeming-so" and therefore to be slightly distrusted. In spring, however, things
are "Perceived by feeling instead of sense" (CP, 214), and this rebirth of feeling
as perception leads to the finding of resemblances—and into summer. Thus all
four seasons operate ironically within themselves and dualistically as a whole.
Each season contains its own possibilities and its own limits; the cycle frees
the poet from his own particular perceptions, allowing him continually to
discover and invent and rediscover.

Yet to read Stevens' poems as "examples" of this (or any) conceptual
ordering would be to reduce them to mere "incidents" in a vague biography
of an idea. One must dissolve any such ordering back into the poems; otherwise
the poems blur and disappear as the ordering sharpens and hardens. The
individual poem is what counts; the coherence between poems is the coherence
of a consistent point of view, which is simply that one's point of view must
be forever shifting. Thus the poems need not refer consistently to a particular
season nor need they refer to any season at all. As Stevens wrote to William
Carlos Williams, "Given a fixed point of view, realistic, imagistic, or what you
will, everything adjusts itself to that point of view; and the process of adjustment is a world in flux, as it should be for a poet." [8] Stevens' "resemblances"
and seasons reflect after all a "process of adjustment," a way of looking at and
thinking about that which is commonly called reality. When Stevens says, "I
am not competent to discuss reality as a philosopher" (OP, 217), he simply
means he is not willing to invent a rigidly ordered région où vivre: just as for
Mallarmé's swan, such an invention would for Stevens be an exil inutile. Any
conceptual ordering of Stevens' poetry must therefore be a possiblity, not an
actuality, because fixing ideas into a pattern remains only a possiblity in the
poetry itself.

Yet it is possible to probe a step further into Stevens' theory of metaphor
to see what precisely generates its nonsystematic nature. Behind Stevens' theory
of metaphor lies a theory of knowledge that, like any epistemology, faces the
question, How do we know? The epistemological problem becomes trouble-
some and difficult when it assumes a split between mind and matter. In his
poetry, Stevens directly confronts this epistemological dualism; and his theory
of metaphor is his solution of it. For Stevens, knowledge derives from the
process of creating metaphor, which is, as noted above, the process of perceiv-

---

8. William Carlos Williams, Selected Essays (New York, 1954), p. 12.

ing resemblances. Knowledge is not a transcendent position that unifies mind and matter into itself; instead, the act of knowing is the act of perceiving a resemblance that holds true for a time—for a "season," Stevens might say. Mind and matter are thus antithetical worlds, but they do not negate one another; and insofar as the mind is capable of perceiving resemblances, and for as long as the mind resists identifying its processes with the fluctuations of matter, metaphor is possible and knowledge is the result.

For Stevens, then, metaphor is both the prelude to knowledge and the evasion of reality. Metaphor becomes the prelude to knowledge when it orders "things as they are" in their uniqueness and isolation into meaningful relationships; it becomes the evasion of reality when these relationships are accepted as the complete and actual description of reality. To see the world only as smothered in a relationship, or to see it only as an assemblage of unique and isolated objects, is for Stevens not to know. But to see the world as both, through metaphor—to move continually between "The bough of summer and the winter branch" (CP, 67)—is to be capable of knowing. Thus Stevens' theory of metaphor is rooted in the epistemological dualism between mind and matter; and metaphor becomes knowledge not in spite of the dualism but because of it.

From *Papers on Language and Literature*, 2 (1966), 57-66.

GEORGE McFADDEN

Poet, Nature, and Society

WALLACE STEVENS disliked miscellany. He waited until he had found his authentic voice before publishing his first volume, which he called *Harmonium* (1923). He was then forty-three years old. In this book Stevens sketches out a conceptual framework which he filled in and extended in the books that followed, with changes in emphasis but without significant changes in outline. The human being as person and poet, the natural world, and society have their places in this framework. To discern its shape, a considerable number of the poems must be read with attention and recollection. For Stevens' meanings do not come to the reader so much through quick insights as by gradual accretion. One does not suddenly grasp his ideas, but rather comes to feel comfortable with a poem which had at first teased and annoyed while it charmed, and whose meaning is the last of its pleasures. It is through a consistent symbolism and a simple but effective myth that the meaning takes form.

A symbol in the verse of Stevens is much more likely to be general than particular. There is almost never a trace of a single event, an actual experience, in his symbols. The particularity of "the dresser of deal, / Lacking the three glass knobs," is only a singular exception to his usual practice. Rather, Stevens sets up an equivalence between a concept and a class of perceptions. The importance of such class-images is less visual than conceptual, for at times the visual element is extremely slight, while the idea itself carries considerable resonance. The most remarkable example is the use of "wigs" and "curls" as symbols in a class of coiffure-images which Stevens employs to express the concept of artificial arrangement in general. The puzzling but important Section VI of "The Comedian as the Letter C," which is subtitled "And Daughters with Curls," in reality has nothing to do with permanents, but rather concerns Stevens' early poetic experiments, that is, his artifices with style. This passage narrates the poet's misguided efforts to bring under stylistic control

> the unbraided femes,
> Green crammers of the green fruits of the world,
> Bidders and biders for its ecstasies,
> True daughters both of Crispin and his clay. (*CP*, 43-44)

The whole section is a comment upon the intensity that went into Stevens' effort of synthesis in unifying reality and poetic expression. On the one hand, there is nature, violent and resisting control, slow to take on any humanly imposed form. On the other, there is human artifice. For the first, Stevens employed a color-symbol, green: "the barbarous green of . . . harsh reality." For the second, he invented the figure of Crispin the hairdresser. Leaving the eighteenth-century world of Bourbon France, Crispin, the "Comedian as the Letter C," valet with his "barber's eye," set sail from Bordeaux for the New World. In Europe the violence of nature had been suppressed and forgotten amid gardens and palaces. The style of Louis XV, which Crispin left behind him, is likely to seem, to Americans at least, the archetype of artificial European elegance—"the wig of things." It expresses a blind continuance in dynastic and social forms that have outlived their date and are ready for violent overthrow. At the same period, "the mountainous coiffures of Bath," the "all-speaking braids" of Utamaro's Japanese courtesans, were keeping the hairdressers busy; but two centuries later this order is utterly decayed: "Alas! Have all the barbers lived in vain / That not one curl in nature has survived?" ("Le Monocle de Mon Oncle," CP, 14).

"Wigs," as standing for an exhausted culture, is perhaps Stevens' most arbitrary symbol; yet it is one of his earliest. In the seven "Poems, 1899-1901" reprinted in the Wallace Stevens number (December, 1940) of the *Harvard Advocate,* we find in "Ballade of the Pink Parasol" the line "Where is the old-time wig." The symbol is reasonable enough when we consider that the United States took form and separated from Europe in the age of wigs. Hence, in the New World, the place for new ideas and forms of civilization, the wig and its curls mean outmoded artifice.

Stevens believed violence to be at the heart of nature (and he introduced Crispin to it in the green jungles of Yucatan). But it is not only the natural environment that is violent. Man as animal, as part of the natural world, has violence at his center. The matching symbol for green, expressing inner human violence, is "the monster":

> Speak of the soul, the mind. It is
> An animal. . . .
>
>   its claws propound, its fangs
> Articulate its desert days.
> ("The Man with the Blue Guitar," CP, 174)

Stevens would control and train the monster in man, but his aim was to "reduce the monster to / Myself " (CP, 175), not to suffocate it. Just as green is always present in nature as a sign of enduring force, but always changing, destroying the old in favor of the new, so in man the monster guarantees vitality and change.

A note which Stevens furnished to Renato Poggioli for his translation into Italian of *The Man with the Blue Guitar (Mattino domenicale ed altre poesie* [Milan, 1954]), indicates the amount of thought Stevens put into his symbols:

The monster—nature, wich [*sic*] I desire to reduce: master, subjugate, acquire complete control over and use freely for my own purpose, as poet. I want, as poet, to be that in nature, which constitutes nature [*sic*] very self. I want to be nature in the form of man, with all the resources of nature. . . . I want, as a man of the imagination, to write poetry with all the power of a monster equal in strength to that of the monster about whom I write. I want man's imagination to be completely adequate in the face of reality. (*CP*, 179)

Stevens' humanism, it can be seen, stopped short of the pretension that nature itself was humane, or that mechanical and planned progress was a possibility. Hence his active scorn of the Soviet attempt to fix a pattern upon mankind. In "A Dish of Peaches in Russia," he suggests that the ripeness of peaches is but one sign of the fundamental untameableness of the world:

> I did not know
> That such ferocities could tear
> One self from another, as these peaches do. (*CP*, 224)

The same idea had already appeared in "The Comedian" (*CP*, 40 ff.).

Even the world of ideas, for Stevens, is violent. He decides the succession of ideas like an old-fashioned anarchist. The poet is a "philosophic assassin" who fires at will and, when the shooting is over, is left alone with one surviving idea; thus "the mass of meaning becomes composed again." The notion has its arbitrary side, but it is linked with Stevens' vitality as a poet. Its serious aspect lies in the immense importance of change to him. "I believe in impermanence" would be the first article of his creed as poet. "The law of chaos is the law of ideas / Of improvisations and seasons of belief" ("Extracts from Addresses to the Academy of Fine Ideas," *CP*, 255).

The world, to Stevens, is protean,

> [a] giant that fought
> Against the murderous alphabet:
>
> The swarm of thoughts, the swarm of dreams
> Of inaccessible Utopia.
>
> A mountainous music always seemed
> To be falling and to be passing away. (*CP*, 179)

The poet, with his "murderous alphabet," fells the giant time after time, but the giant will not stay down.

This metaphysical view determined one of Stevens' most striking qualities of style, his remarkably tentative use of metaphor. He did not believe that the world was a work of art where all metaphor could crisscross in a divinely ordained pattern. He distrusted metaphor, even while he used it (just as he distrusted the imagination's blue), because it pretended to be permanent. On "a level where everything is poetic," he said, a statement "produced in the imagination a universal iridescence, a dithering of presences and, say, a complex of differences."[1] The word "dithering" appealed to him: he used it to mean a shimmering, a shifting of perspective that was true to changing nature even while it caught and held the eye. Insisting that imagination must add something, rather than pretend to assert an already existing identity, he preferred proximate comparisons—"as if," "the way," "for example"—to the direct metaphor.

For the nobler aims of poetry, especially, metaphor is not enough. It leaves experience with nothing added except a perishing allusion or relation. In "Add This to Rhetoric," Stevens suggests that nature is like a model needing to be posed before the artist can go ahead. Poetic imagination must add the sense, the meaning, to nature, and thus "create the pose." After this first stage of reconstruction of the outside world, the poet goes on, as "countryman" or "paysan," to create a countryside composed in the imagination and the feelings. He will die crying out that

> with our bones
> We left much more, left what still is
> The look of things, left what we felt
> At what we saw.
> ("A Postcard from the Volcano," CP, 159)

That a landscape might be posed, in particular, as a symbolic "woman in the air" seems to have been a habitual notion with Stevens. This "woman" seems to be present in the early "Paltry Nude Starts on a Spring Voyage" (CP, 5), as well as in the immature but attractive "Apostrophe to Vincentine," where we read "Monotonous earth I saw become / Illimitable spheres of you" (CP, 53). No longer sentimental, the notion is firmly established in "The Idea of Order at Key West," which begins "She sang beyond the genius of the sea." "She" is the idea of order, a kind of *genius loci*, the "single artificer of the world / In which she sang." The sea was "merely a place by which she walked to sing" (CP, 128-29). The poet, as a thinking, feeling man, is in continuous search for this woman. Usually she symbolizes the primitive fecundity of nature: "Green is the night . . . / Like a noble figure, out of the sky . . . / The abstract, the archaic queen" ("The Candle a Saint," CP, 223); "the softest woman . . . reality, / The gross, the fecund" ("Esthétique du Mal," CP, 321-22).

In "Notes Toward a Supreme Fiction," Stevens took cognizance of this

---

1. *OP*, 192. Whitehead's philosophy gave Stevens much encouragement. Cf. "Sea Surface Full of Clouds" and Whitehead's "a sense-object perceived at one time is a distinct object from a sense-object seen at another time. Thus the sight . . . at noon is distinct from its sight at 12:30." *The Aims of Education*, Mentor Book (New York, 1949), p. 128.

symbolic figure and gave her a formally mythic stature already implicit in the
Harmonium poems. He began by positing along with "the first idea," a concept
which he himself explained as meaning the world without varnish or surface
coating,[2] an "immaculate beginning"—the appearance of man to confront the
world of nonhuman being (*CP*, 382). He accepts Adam, standing for the rational
in man and Eve, standing for the emotional. Then, he writes,

> Eve made air the mirror of herself,
> Of her sons and of her daughters. They found themselves
> In heaven as in a glass; a second earth.

Stevens relies upon this Eve-figure, the woman in the air, to join symbolically
the two earths, just as imagination mediates between the violence of being and
the joy of reality, that is, between matter and spirit. She appears again in "Notes
Toward a Supreme Fiction" as Nazia Nunzio (*CP*, 395). This odd name,
obviously cognate to "Annunziazione," links her with the figure of the Virgin
Mary, as did the earlier reference to the "immaculate beginning." The Eve-
Mary figure of Stevens is linked, as her spouse, not to the Holy Spirit (as the
Blessed Virgin was at the Annunciation), but to the human spirit:

> I am the woman stripped more nakedly
> Than nakedness, standing before an inflexible
> Order, saying I am the contemplated spouse.
>
> Speak to me that, which spoken, will array me
> In its own only precious ornament.
> Set on me the spirit's diamond coronal. (*CP*, 396)

The Eve-Mary figure appears a third time and with another name in a better-
known passage of this same poem. Once again there is an evocation of the
Gospels:

> There was a mystic marriage in Catawba,
> At noon it was on the mid-day of the year
> Between a great captain and the maiden Bawda. (*CP*, 401)

Perhaps, indeed, there is a trace of natural mysticism in this female figure.
In "Things of August" Stevens seems to be making a rare reference to a
historical personal experience. After these lines:

2. In an unpublished letter to Henry Church, Oct. 28, 1942, quoted by Michel Benamou, "Sur
le prétendu 'Symbolisme' de Wallace Stevens," *Critique*, XVII (December, 1961), 1037. On the
implications of "the first idea" see Frank Doggett, "This Invented World: Stevens' 'Notes Toward
a Supreme Fiction,'" *ELH*, XXVIII (1961), 286. Doggett uses the apt term "personifications" for
what I call myth.

> The rich earth, of its own self made rich,
> Fertile of its own leaves and days and wars,
> Of its brown wheat rapturous in the wind,
> The nature of its women in the air, (*CP*, 491)

he goes on to recall an almost Dedalian epiphany:

> When was it that we heard the voice of union?
>
> Was it as we sat in the park and the archaic form
> Of a woman with a cloud on her shoulder rose.
> Against the trees. . . . (*CP*, 494)

Other evocations of the woman in the air appear in expressions such as "earth seen as inamorata" (*CP*, 484), "the desired" (*CP*, 505), and especially the closing lines (before the postscript) of "Notes Toward a Supreme Fiction":

> Fat girl, terrestrial, my summer, my night,
> . . . . .
> The fiction that results from feeling. Yes, that.
>
> They will get it straight one day at the Sorbonne.
> We shall return at twilight from the lecture
> Pleased that the irrational is rational,
>
> Until flicked by feeling, in a gildered street,
> I call you by name, my green, my fluent mundo.
> You will have stopped revolving except in crystal. (*CP*, 406-407)

Here Stevens seems to be dealing, very guardedly, with the Hegelian view that the "more than rational distortion" of poetry would eventually give way to rational, scientific statement. But such progress is possible only if the exceptional insights of individuals become habitual for society as a whole.

Some of the postures that art imposes upon nature are more durable than others. Sometimes the human imagination has created what seems to be "an image that was mistress of the world" ("A Golden Woman in a Silver Mirror"). In that case mankind, freed from gropings of the spirit for a time, would see a world which "will have stopped revolving except in crystal." For the individual, of course, such permanence is short-lived—"dark death is the breaking of a glass"—but societies are made glorious for long periods of time by their mistress-images:

> But the images, disembodied, are not broken.
> They have, or they may have, their glittering crown,
> Sound-soothing pearl and omni-diamond,

Of the most beautiful, the most beautiful maid
And mother. How long have you lived and looked,
Ababba, expecting this king's queen to appear? (*CP,* 460-61)

Our society, for its own mistress-image, awaits a Bernard, an Aquinas, a Dante, an Angelico, to conceive her. Deferentially, Stevens offers his "fat girl," his Bawda.

The creatures of feeling and imagination exist in a transparent element, as if in air. When conceived in feeling and given the force of love, as by the artist, Stevens thought of them as possessing an essential, exemplary power, perspicuous to the consciousness as glass is to the sun. They would appeal to the rational in man, not the superstitious. Belief in the possible existence of a race of men formed by such images preserved Stevens' hope for humanity:

> The impossible possible philosophers' man,
> The man who has had the time to think enough,
> The central man, the human globe, responsive
> As a mirror with a voice, the man of glass,
> Who in a million diamonds sums us up.
> ("Asides on the Oboe," *CP,* 250)

He admits that "final belief / Must be in a fiction," but declares that, unlike the dead fictions of religion, the rational fictions of philosophy can still inspire the feelings and the imagination: "The philosophers' man alone still walks in dew." Here, in "dew," Stevens recurs to the symbol used long before, in "Sunday Morning" and in "The Comedian as the Letter C," to mean the freshness of the creative imagination.[3]

Freshness of impulse in the artist may give expression to this "central man," the "man of glass," but no one else will understand or share the artist's feelings except through an individual imaginative development. The quality of one's perception is paramount; we must pass beyond ordinary vision to see "the reality / Of the other eye" before any of us can become

> the meta-men for whom
> The world has turned to the several speeds of glass,
>
> For whom no blue in the sky prevents them, as
> They understand, and take on potency,
> By growing clear, transparent magistrates,
>
> Bearded with chains of blue-green glitterings
> And wearing hats of angular flick and fleck,
> Cold with an under impotency that they know,

---

3. Frank Kermode, *Wallace Stevens* (New York, 1961), p. 42, points out the connection between "dew" and the "earthly origin and destination" of man.

Now that they know, because they know. One comes
To the things of medium nature, as meta-men
Behold them, not choses of Provence, growing

In glue, but things transfixed, transpierced and well
Perceived: the white seen smoothly argentine
And plated up, dense silver shine, in a land

Without a god, O silver sheen and shape,
And movement of emotion through the air,
True nothing, yet accosted self to self.
("The Bouquet," *CP*, 449)

In this poem, symbolically one of his richest, perhaps Stevens meant to oppose to the "things" of the Sartrean existentialists, absurdly alien to man, the essentialism of Santayana, according to which things are knowable in their ideas when properly perceived. But what he chooses to emphasize is not ideas or essences, but emotion, "movement of emotion through the air . . . accosted self to self"; emotion which may have been learned through the mistress-images of one's culture, but which is, nevertheless, a spontaneous generation of the individual self.

The symbolic complexity of the passage just quoted illustrates Stevens' method of imbuing ideas with feeling. "Meta-men" means the men of the future, the higher evolutionary type, as well as the men who see beyond both the deadness of commonplace being and the exhaustion of states of feeling based on the imagination of the past (blue). They approach the clearness of glass as they take on reality. They become intellectual leaders of the people (magistrates; or, elsewhere, rabbis, scholars). They are vested with dignity and status (bearded). But they are not hieratic figures; their dignity is due to a habit of mind which has, in their case, held fast, even in imagination, to the violence and instability of being (blue-green glitterings). They are cold because their knowledge has begun where human wisdom begins, in the first icy stasis of primeval being, and is cherished in "poverty," or intellectual *ascesis*.[4]

Evolutionary hope in Stevens is not biological. He looks, not for the superman or the master-man, but for "major man"; not an individual, not even an imaginary figure, but a principle, an exponent (in the mathematical sense) of an abstraction. He is "part of the commonal." There is nothing divine about him, though the romantics, "beau linguists," once found the idiom of apotheosis for man:

But apotheosis is not
The origin of major man. He comes,

4. I think Kermode might have mentioned (p. 39) the positive, preparatory function of Stevens' "poverty." In this respect it is more than the mere "absence of imaginative happiness."

Compact in invincible foils, from reason,
Lighted at midnight by the studious eye,
Swaddled in revery. . . .
                    ("Notes Toward a Supreme Fiction," *CP*, 387-88)

Stevens' major man is lifted out of mere nature, not by divine fatherhood (note
the Gospel reference in "swaddled"), nor by his own will, nor even perhaps
by his intelligence; but, most of all, through his feelings, his sense of beauty
and the enjoyment it brings.

Whistle aloud, too weedy wren. I can
Do all that angels can. I enjoy like them,
Like men besides. . . . (*CP*, 405)

Stevens' final vision is of a fully human society, which has found its "imago,"
its abstract major man to act as its principle, and which is peopled by "medium
man"—ordinary mortals, neither scholarly nor creative in an exceptional way,
but led on to nobility by the satisfaction they take, living in a land formed by
thinkers and artists:

Medium man
In February hears the imagination's hymns
And sees its images, its motions
And multitude of motions

And feels the imagination's mercies,
In a season more than sun and south wind. . . . ("Imago," *CP*, 439)

Stevens has a message for society, but it is addressed to the individual. Medium
man is the common man who has gained the gift of vision, has become a
medium, so to say, through whom everyday, ordinary life is transpierced by
the imagination and its sense of beauty. This individual, inward renewal, the
ennobling of the quotidian, is his hope.

From *Modern Language Quarterly*, 23 (1962), 263-71.

GEORGE S. LENSING

Stevens' Letters of Rock and Water

IN ONE of his *Adagia*, Stevens affirms: "Life is an affair of people not of places. But for me life is an affair of places and that is the trouble." The fecundity of imagination perhaps most manifests itself by fixing upon place in Stevens' poems, and the settings of Florida and the tropics, of European and Oriental locations, are regular in his verse. This admission by Stevens is remarkable when one learns that Stevens never left the U.S. except for a couple of brief visits to Havana and a trip to California by way of the Panama Canal. It was through his active interest in foreign environments and cultures, nurtured by extensive reading, that Stevens was to discover other areas of the world; it was also through letters: "Ceylon is the sort of place with which one can come to grips and still be fascinated. It is like Florida, or, to take something a little more prodigious, like Bengal, as I understand Bengal to be."[1] The tone of this letter to Leonard C. van Geyzel, who lived in Ceylon, is repeated in another to Barbara Church in France: "The postcards from Ville d'Avray came the other day. They did me a lot of good. In fact, I survive on postcards from Europe" (*L*, 797). It was with a half dozen correspondents living in various parts of the world that Stevens exchanged letters for years and through whom he received a regular stream of artifacts, books, jewelry, scrolls, volumes of poetry, teas, spices, and jellies. Stevens' interest in these cultures was constant and his friendships prospered, resulting in hundreds of letters, even though in individual cases he had not personally met the correspondent and in all cases did not see them often. This correspondence personalized and vitalized alien parts of the world for Stevens and provided a store from which the poetic imagination could generously draw. A major value of the *Letters* is that they reveal for the first time these sources.

In several ways, the correspondence with Thomas McGreevy, an Irish poet and art critic, is typical. The epistolary friendship began in 1948, when McGreevy established a contact with Stevens; they exchanged correspondence regularly for the remainder of Stevens' life, though they met, apparently, only once, the year before Stevens' death. McGreevy's interest in poetry and art was a natural basis for friendship and he was later to become, to Stevens' delight, director of the National Gallery in Dublin, but there was also a certain exuberance in the McGreevy letters that Stevens enjoyed, as he commented to

1. *Letters of Wallace Stevens*, selected and edited by Holly Stevens (New York, 1966), 353. This book will hereafter be referred to as *L*.

Barbara Church: "He is, in any event, a blessed creature, sustained by a habit of almost medieval faith and I like the God bless you with which he winds up his letters . . . " (L, 682-83).

It was through the McGreevy correspondence that Stevens came to write "Our Stars Come from Ireland" in 1948. The poem was written at a time when Ireland had been brought vividly to life in Stevens' imagination, as he expressed in another letter to Mrs. Church: "The Irish seem to have hearts. Besides, Dublin and the whole place look to my eye like the pages of a novel—not one of those frightful continental novels in ten volumes, all psychology and no fresh air, but a novel full of the smell of ale and horses and noisy with people living in flats, playing the piano, and telephoning and with the sound of drunks in the street at night" (L, 609). The first part of the poem is addressed to McGreevy: *"Tom McGreevy, in America, Thinks of Himself as a Boy."* The poem itself, as Stevens says to McGreevy, celebrates the importance of places in the past as figments of memory:

> Over the top of the Bank of Ireland,
> The wind blows quaintly
> Its thin-stringed music,
> As he heard it in Tarbert. (CP, 454)

The stars of Ireland, of Tarbert and Kerry and Mal Bay, move westward (Part II of the poem is entitled *"The Westwardness of Everything."*) and hover over the Pennsylvania landscape of Stevens' own youth, resulting in a harmony, "These Gaeled and fitful-fangled darknesses / Made suddenly luminous" (CP, 455).

José Rodríguez Feo, a Cuban, was a recent graduate of Harvard when he wrote Stevens in 1944 requesting permission to translate "Esthétique du Mal" for a little magazine, *Origenes*, he had founded in Havana. Little more than a year later *Origenes* introduced Wallace Stevens to Cubans in Spanish. Stevens' correspondence with Rodríguez Feo, as in the case with McGreevy, expanded to include a variety of subjects. His new friend was able to introduce Stevens to the work of a number of Cuban artists, particularly the drawings of Mariano, exhibitions of whom Stevens visited occasionally in New York City. Their letters could also touch on the more mundane, including Rodríguez Feo's description of his family life in Cuba and his mother's burro, Pompilio, in whom Stevens took a spirited interest: "There still remains in Cuba a nice old woman who loves her burro and asks José to tell me, for Xmas, that Pompilio is well. Saludos, Pompilio" (L, 865).

"The Novel" was conceived from such a Cuban setting provided by Rodríguez Feo, and the protagonist of the poem is one "José" from "vividest Varadero," the beach-site from which much of his correspondence with Stevens originated. What is especially notable is the fact that the third and fourth stanzas of the poem are almost literal transcriptions of a plea made by the mother of Rodríguez Feo to prevent her son from accepting a position with

UNESCO in Paris. The Cuban quotes his mother in a letter to Stevens on September 21, 1948:

> . . . I gave up the job at the Unesco at Paris because mother was afraid I would freeze in the Parisian hotels. She happened to listen in on a conversation wherein a friend of mine described in gruesome details the fate of an Argentine writer. At night he would go to bed, cover himself with blankets—protruding from the pile of wool a hand, in a black glove, holds a novel by Camus. That was the only safe way he could keep in touch with French literary events. Mother was much impressed by the picture of the engloved hand holding a trembling little volume. She begged me to stay away. (*L*, 617)

Stevens was obviously taken by the description of the Argentine writer, who is drawn into the poem "verbatim from your letter":

> *Mother was afraid I should freeze in the Parisian hotels.*
> *She had heard of the fate of an Argentine writer. At night,*
> *He would go to bed, cover himself with blankets—*
>
> *Protruding from the pile of wool, a hand,*
> *In a black glove, holds a novel by Camus. She begged*
> *That I stay away.* These are the words of José . . . (*CP*, 457)

The poem continues by describing the sound of the water at Varadero Beach:

> How tranquil it was at vividest Varadero,
> While the water kept running through the mouth of the speaker,
> Saying: *Olalla blanca en el blanco.* . . . (*CP*, 457)

The quotation from Lorca in the last line of the tercet, interestingly enough, had come to Stevens through a letter by Thomas McGreevy a few months earlier, as Stevens acknowledged to McGreevy in a letter at the time of the appearance of the poem in *The Auroras of Autumn*: "Also, in the poem called *The Novel* I use a line from Lorca which you quoted." (*L*, 690). The poem itself goes on to describe the fear born of the "Arcadian imagination" which had taken hold of the Argentine. At the end, the Argentine has been enlarged to include all men. "The Novel" does not geographically focus on Havana, which Stevens knew first hand, but Varadero, which he knew only through the letters and postcards of Rodríguez Feo. The background of this poem and the circumstances out of which it came to be written are perhaps the best illustration of one of the poem's principal conclusions: "Only the real can be / Unreal today, be hidden and alive" (*CP*, 458).

Rodríguez Feo had played a part in two earlier poems by Stevens, one of which bears the name of his correspondent-friend, "A Word with José Rodríguez-Feo." This poem, as Stevens explained to him after writing the poem, insists that "although the grotesque has taken possession of the sub-conscious, this is not because there is any particular relationship between the two things" (*L*, 489). Thus, the answer to the question posed in the poem, "Is lunar Habana the Cuba of the self?" (*CP*, 333), is negative. The grotesque is separate, a "simplified geography, in which / The sun comes up like news from Africa" (*CP*, 334).

A third poem, "Paisant Chronicle," was written by Stevens as a response to a number of questions about what constituted the "major men," an appellation which Rodríguez Feo had noted in earlier poems like "Notes toward a Supreme Fiction." In several letters Stevens attempted to clarify his idea, undoubtedly stirring his own interest in the subject of the hero-giant-poet that remained a continuing feature of many of Stevens' poems. In one letter to his Cuban friend, for example, he declares that the "major men" are neither "exponents of humanism" nor "Nietzschean shadows." Rather, they are the creators of the supreme fiction which Stevens defined as "some arbitrary object of belief"(*L*, 485). Stevens considered the hero-figure as the man who could make prevail the fictions which men can accept and by which they can live their lives: "The major men are part of the entourage of that artificial object." Stevens was dissatisfied with this prose exegesis—as he was with all the paraphrasing of the ideas of his poetry reproduced in the *Letters*. A more fruitful attempt to define "major men" was through a poem, and in "Paisant Chronicle," Stevens wrote to Rodríguez Feo, "I have defined major men for you" (*L*, 489).

In this poem, Stevens distinguishes major men from traditional national heroes and other men who are admired for feats of bravery. The major man is different, embodying the paradox that is at the heart of all of Stevens' poetry. He is real enough to be believable, but he is also the man of imagination, the embellisher of reality. He is real and unreal and, as a result, ideal and basically impossible to be realized. As the poem itself declares, major men are "beyond / Reality" but "composed thereof"; "They are / The fictive man created out of men" (*CP*, 335). As a result, the major men can bring to life the fictions of the imagination, without which no man can survive, but, at the same time, they do not compromise the undistorted reality, without which all fictions are evasive. Like the "central man" of an earlier poem, "Asides on the Oboe," the major man is "the impossible possible philosophers' man, / . . . Who in a million diamonds sums us up" (*CP*, 250).

The long exchange of letters between Stevens and Rodriguez Feo was to have major implications for Stevens' poetry—not only providing settings or even, in the case of "The Novel," almost a literal phraseology for poems, but also a source of stimulation in regard to major concepts in Stevens' long poetic elaboration. The coming to terms with the "major men" is an incisive example of the latter.

In 1937, at the suggestion of mutual friends, Stevens wrote to Leonard C. van Geyzel in Ceylon, asking him to send some carvings, jewelry, and tea as Christmas gifts for his family. Van Geyzel was able to respond to the request and the poet in Hartford was elated with the quality and taste of the selections. An exchange of letters ensued, frequently accompanied by books and other articles. It was through van Geyzel that Ceylon was to take on a prominent symbolic import in Stevens' own imagination and, consequently, in his poems. Some nineteen months after the correspondence began, for example, Stevens reported to van Geyzel: "Ceylon has taken a strong hold on my imagination. These things [other articles sent by van Geyzel] help one to visualize the people in the streets" (*L*, 337). It was also at this time that references to Ceylon began to appear in Stevens' poems, usually as representations of the colorings of the imagination. One of the first, in "Connoisseur of Chaos," was written about four months after Stevens received the original Christmas package from van Geyzel. Here the allusion to the fact that "Englishmen lived without tea in Ceylon" (*CP*, 215) appears as one in a series of illustrations showing that "inherent opposites" can create an "essential unity." In another poem written later, "Extracts from Addresses to the Academy of Fine Ideas," Ceylon is described as a "past apocalypse" (*CP*, 257) which the mind, at last poetically satisfied, can discard. Or, in "Description Without Place," the frequently cited reference to "Pablo Neruda in Ceylon" (*CP*, 341) illustrates the transforming power of the imagination: "Things are as they seemed." One of the most exotic references to the island off the southeastern coast of India occurs in "Notes toward a Supreme Fiction" where Ceylon is an example of imaginative sound and color:

> The elephant
> Breaches the darkness of Ceylon with blares,
>
> The glitter-goes on surfaces of tanks,
> Shattering velvetest far-away (*CP*, 384).

As in the case of Ireland and Cuba, Ceylon eventually took on dynamic and multi-faceted contours in the poetry of Stevens. Ceylon, like Ireland, was never known first hand by Stevens, but through the van Geyzel correspondence which continued for some eighteen years, Stevens came to know it with imaginative immediacy.

Sister M. Bernetta Quinn was an early and avid critic of Stevens' verse, and, after sending a commentary of his poems to which he, in turn, responded, she began the practice of sending greeting cards at Christmas and Easter. One card, dispatched during the Easter season in 1949, included a reference to the lion of Juda. Stevens later acknowledged, "I put the lion into something that I was doing at the time" (*L*, 635). The poem was "An Ordinary Evening in New Haven." Here he recognizes the endurance of the religious image: "We remember the lion of Juda and we save / The phrase . . . " (*CP*, 472). The lion, however, is metamorphosed into a cat, "potent in the sun" (*CP*, 473), thus reducing the religious reference to the level of common reality: "And Juda becomes New Haven or else must."

Another poem also originated from a card. John Sweeney, director of the poetry room in the Lamont Library at Harvard, had been interested in Stevens' work and had arranged for an exhibition of his books in 1951. The following year, while vacationing in Ireland, he sent Stevens a postcard with a photograph of the Cliffs of Moher in County Clare. The majestic sweep of the cliffs, "like a gust of freedom, a return to the spacious, solitary world in which we used to exist" (L, 760-61), provided Stevens with a setting for poetic exploration. As he wrote later to Mrs. Church, the photograph "eventually became a poem" (L, 770).

The poem itself, "The Irish Cliffs of Moher," a short lyric in couplets and free verse, conceives of the cliffs as ancient and "Above the real" (CP, 501). They become a symbol of solidarity between present and past and are transformed into the image of the father: "A likeness, one of the race of fathers: earth / And sea and air" (CP, 502).

It is clear from a reading of the Letters that many of the ideas which were to emerge in Stevens' prose essays and criticism were also earlier formulated and refined through his correspondence. This is particularly so in the letters to Ronald Latimer, Hi Simons, Henry Church, and José Rodríguez Feo.

Latimer, for example, was a rather enigmatic man who, according to Stevens, eventually "turned Buddhist" and became "a monk or priest in one of the temples at Tokio" (L, 391). Stevens himself loyally defended Latimer who, as editor of the Alcestis Press, published two volumes of poetry by Stevens, Ideas of Order in 1935 and Owl's Clover in 1936. One of the subjects of the epistolary exchange was the role of romanticism in modern poetry, and, even though in his own work Stevens was to participate in the reaction against many of the most extreme tenets of romanticism, he was also anxious to defend his own interpretation of it. To Latimer in March, 1935, for example, he spoke of romanticism, distinct from its "pejorative sense" (L, 277), as something "constantly new" through which "the most casual things take on transcendence." The embellishments of the poetic imagination, according to Stevens, were always recognized as manifestations of the romantic in a positive sense. Two weeks after elaborating on the theory of romanticism in the letter to Latimer, Stevens agreed tentatively to do a review of the poetry of Marianne Moore, whom he recognized as an example of the "new romantic" (L, 279). In writing the review itself, "A Poet that Matters," Stevens repeated the concept that he had worked out with Latimer in relation to Marianne Moore's poetry: "Yes, but for the romantic in its other sense, meaning always the living and at the same time the imaginative, the youthful, the delicate and a variety of things which it is not necessary to try to particularize at the moment, constitutes the vital element in poetry. It is absurd to wince at being called a romantic poet. Unless one is that, one is not a poet at all " (OP, 251-52).

In this larger sense, the originality and freshness of the imagination always constitute the highest form of the romantic. "Just as there is always a romantic that is potent, so there is always a romantic that is impotent," says Stevens in one of the Adagia (OP, 180).

To Latimer also, Stevens elaborated upon the seriousness and indispensability of poetry and art for all men, a concept that was to become the basis of his justification of the imagination. In a letter to him later in 1935, Stevens spoke of the value of poetry, and thus of the imagination, as the only valid "sanction" in life: "I really ought not to answer a question like your question in regard to the status of poetry without thinking about it carefully, but, offhand, I think that the real trouble with poetry is that poets have no conception of the importance of the thing. Life without poetry is, in effect, life without a sanction. Poetry does not only mean verse; in a way it means painting, it means the theatre and all the rest of it" (*L*, 299). This principle, relating to the value of the artistic imagination, was, of course, to be a kind of touchstone in all of Stevens' poetry and prose. What is significant here is that, through his correspondence, Stevens discovered an invaluable means for framing his ideas, "thinking about it carefully." The essay, "The Noble Rider and the Sound of Words," originally read at Princeton in 1941, is essentially an elaboration upon the same idea of the social function of the poet. The poet, he says, is to provide for society its necessary sanctions: "I think that his function is to make his imagination theirs and that he fulfills himself only as he sees his imagination become the light in the minds of others. His role, in short, is to help people to live their lives."

The *Letters*, in addition to providing immediate sources for both his poetry and prose, also fill in a great deal of information about other sources and influences. Almost certainly the source for the poem "Nuns Painting Water-Lilies" is disclosed in a 1948 letter to Barbara Church: "Often instead of walking downtown I walk in the little park through which you drove when you were here. Until quite lately a group of nuns came there each morning to paint water colors especially of the water lilies" (*L*, 610).

Another poem, "Angel Surrounded by Paysans," was taken from a title Stevens had personally applied to a Tal Coat painting which had been sent to him from France: "I have even given it a title of my own: *Angel Surrounded By Peasants*. The angel is the Venetian glass bowl on the left with the little spray of leaves in it. The peasants are the terrines, bottles and the glasses that surround it" (*L*, 649-50). "The Owl in the Sacrophagus" ("This is the mythology of modern death. . . . " [*CP*, 435]) was written after the death of Henry Church, one of Stevens' favorite correspondents and the man to whom he dedicated "Notes toward a Supreme Fiction." Stevens' practice, in the twenties and thirties, of making an annual business and pleasure trip to Miami or Key West with Judge Arthur Powell provided the background for the large number of poems relating to Florida. Another long and rather fatiguing business trip through Tennessee in 1918 may well have suggested the popular "Anecdote of the Jar" ("I placed a jar in Tennessee . . . " [*CP*, 76]). "Sea Surface Full of Clouds" was definitely inspired by the boat trip in 1923 with Mrs. Stevens through the Panama Canal and past the Gulf of Tehuantepec off southern Mexico.

The ultimate value of a close study of Stevens' letters, however, is not to seek out various influences on his work, nor to apply slavishly his prose paraphrases for previously written poems. Rather, the perusal of the *Letters* as the actual workshop for the creation of his poetry, the means by which poems originated and took form, yields their unique and most fascinating significance. In this sense, Stevens' letters have a dimension not found in those of most poet-correspondents. Letters introduced Stevens to the world—geographically and imaginatively—and much of the brio and panache of his work is rooted in these exchanges. Finally, it was surety bonds and letters from Ceylon, both of which, on a given morning, Stevens found on his desk, that made up his own most immediate world of reality and imagination.

From *Essays in Honor of Esmond Linworth Marilla,* ed. Thomas A. Kirby and William John Olive (Baton Rouge: Louisiana State Univ. Press, 1970), pp. 321-30.

WILLIAM W. BEVIS

The Arrangement of *Harmonium*

Harmonium is a delightfully perverse book, for in it Stevens placed his most dissimilar poems side by side. Critics have often noted certain types of contrast within single Stevens poems—such ironies as muscular chefs and "flowers in last month's newspapers"—and Stevens' exaggeration of these ironies through obscure conceptions, strange visions and bizarre diction:

> Call the roller of big cigars,
> The muscular one, and bid him whip
> In kitchen cups concupiscent curds.
> Let the wenches dawdle in such dress
> As they are used to wear, and let the boys
> Bring flowers in last month's newspapers.
> ("The Emperor of Ice-Cream")

But contrasts arise between the poems of *Harmonium* as well as within them. By juxtaposing different subjects, styles and assumptions, by placing recent poems in between old ones like "flowers in last month's newspapers," Stevens extended his use of novelty, whimsy and contrast from individual poems to their arrangement in his book.

The contrasts produced by the arrangement of the poems in *Harmonium* are of all kinds: antitheses, contradictions, changes of tone or subtle deflections of points of view may delight and confuse the reader. But while many types of contrast appear in the book, adjacent poems are usually contrasted in some single specific way. In order to understand how *Harmonium* was put together, how its arrangement may affect our reading, and what aid a critic may derive from other printings of *Harmonium* poems, let us examine the extraordinarily clear contrast which arises between "Banal Sojourn" and "Depression before Spring," poems adjacent in *Harmonium* which call for different responses to the word "green":

Banal Sojourn

Two wooden tubs of blue hydrangeas stand at the foot of the stone steps.
The sky is a blue gum streaked with rose. The trees are black.
The grackles crack their throats of bone in the smooth air.
Moisture and heat have swollen the garden into a slum of bloom.
Pardie! Summer is like a fat beast, sleepy in mildew,

Our old bane, green and bloated, serene, who cries,
"That bliss of stars, that princox of evening heaven!" reminding of seasons,
When radiance came running down, slim through the bareness.
And so it is one damns that green shade at the bottom of the land.
For who can care at the wigs despoiling the Satan ear?
And who does not seek the sky unfuzzed, soaring to the princox?
One has a malady, here, a malady. One feels a malady.

Depression before Spring

The cock crows
But no queen rises.

The hair of my blonde
Is dazzling,
As the spittle of cows
Threading the wind.

Ho! Ho!

But ki-ki-ri-ki
Brings no rou-cou,
No rou-cou-cou.

But no queen comes
In slipper green.

The obvious contrasts of long and short lines, of emotive and austere diction and syntax, are augmented by apparently conflicting uses of an image: "green" in "Banal Sojourn" is a simple and strong image of despicable rank growth, but in the next poem, "Depression before Spring," the same color is hardly loathsome. We know the queen "In slipper green" is desired; she is invited by the "Depression" title, the plaintive quality of the three "buts," and the unanswered call in the next to the last stanza. The queen seems to represent an answer to some malady; "green" here, instead of imaging a malady as it does in "Banal Sojourn," in "Depression before Spring" implies its cure.

Approached alone, each poem presents particular difficulties. "Banal Sojourn" is a fairly direct reaction against "Summer . . . sleepy in mildew, / Our old bane, green and bloated." The statement is obvious, but the choice of images seems capricious and perhaps inadequate. Why does summer remind us of "That bliss of stars, the princox of the evening heaven" and its ambiguous "seasons"? Would not a winter scene or the radiance of early spring be a more appropriate antidote to the malady of summer grossness? Stars are present, radiant and beautiful during all seasons, especially summer. That the poem opposes a "green shade" to a star is apparent, but that opposition should be expressed in those terms seems forced. The imagery appears unnatural.

"Depression before Spring" presents a critic with greater difficulties. Some solution or relief to a "Depression before Spring" is imaged by a queen, "In slipper green," who will answer the cry of the cock. We immediately think that the queen is spring itself, which will end winter's discontent, but this does not satisfactorily explain the second and third stanzas. Why does he compare his blonde's hair to "the spittle of cows," and then laugh?

Nor are the two poems mutually illuminating. When a poem is obscure, especially if the quality of an image or symbol is in doubt, we look to other works by the poet. While there is no reason to demand consistency, we do expect certain similarities which mark the various poems as the products of a single mind. In Stevens' case, we find the poems stamped by recurrent themes and an amazing and particular talent with words—his diction and sound identify him—but the attempt to read one poem in the light of another may be quite misleading, especially when adjacent poems of *Harmonium* are involved. Ronald Sukenick, in his recent guide *Wallace Stevens: Musing the Obscure* (New York, 1967), yields to the desire to make Stevens consistent and to reconcile adjacent poems in *Harmonium;* he refers both "Banal Sojourn" and "Depression before Spring" to the following statements:

Nor, correspondingly, is fulfillment itself absolutely good, as in "Banal Sojourn" (*CP,* 62), where the fulfillment of summer is described as having become a surfeit. This pattern is repeated in the cycle of the seasons as they affect the emotions, with winter representing barrenness, spring, desire, summer, fulfillment, and autumn, the decay of desire, a kind of asceticism. The beginning of each emotional season is an experience of freshness and the end one of ennui and impatience for change. . . . (*CP,* 7)

Although such seasonal symbolism definitely occurs in Stevens' work, if we rest content with this pleasingly consistent symbolism we fall into an easy but misleading interpretation of the two poems: "green" equals growth, which is rare before spring and therefore desired but too abundant in summer and therefore hated. Such an interpretation seems plausible, if one approaches the poems in their *Harmonium* context and tries to explain them both by a single rationale, yet it does not do justice to either poem or explain their particular perplexities: why is the "green shade" opposed to a star and what is the meaning of the second stanza of "Depression before Spring"? "Green" must suggest more than leaves which we welcome or abhor according to the law of supply and demand.

But the reader may seek aid outside of the poems themselves and outside of *Harmonium.* Sixty-seven of the seventy-four poems of the 1923 *Harmonium*[1] had first been published in small magazines between 1914 and 1923, most in groups of two or more. Such "groups" varied tremendously in character, from

1. Since the 1931 *Harmonium* contained almost entirely the same poems in the same order, augmented by fourteen additional poems placed in a block near the end, the 1931 *Harmonium* reprinted in *Collected Poems* is for present purposes a suitable replica of the 1923 edition.

"Two poems by Wallace Stevens," each titled, obviously a printing of two quite separate poems accepted by the editor and published adjacent, to "Phases," a titled group of four untitled war poems, numbered one through four, which exhibit a clear progression and interdependence.

These varied original groups have one common characteristic: each is homogeneous, unified by a fairly consistent theme, tone or poetics. Although Stevens arranged *Harmonium* by juxtaposing dissimilar poems, he had previously gathered similar poems into each of his groups. The original groups therefore offer us a different context, also created by the author (although sometimes modified by his editors), in which we can read most of the poems of *Harmonium.*

"Banal Sojourn" was first reprinted in "Pecksniffiana" (October, 1919, *Poetry*), a large titled group of fourteen poems. We do not know exactly how or why the group was formed—in all probability it was simply made up of poems recently written or revised—but we do find in letters that Wallace Stevens substituted a few poems and dropped others, and requested a certain order for the poems which Harriet Monroe almost followed. Miss Monroe printed this group:

> Fabliau of Florida
> Homunculus et la Belle Etoile
> The Weeping Burgher
> Peter Parasol
> Exposition of the Contents of a Cab
> Ploughing on Sunday
> Banal Sojourn
> The Indigo Glass in the Grass
> Anecdote of the Jar
> Of the Surface of Things
> The Curtains in the House of the Metaphysician
> The Place of the Solitaires
> The Paltry Nude Starts on a Spring Voyage
> Colloquy with a Polish Aunt

Two images, and the concepts they suggest, unify the "Pecksniffiana" group and represent the poles of concrete and abstract, reality and imagination: "bare" suggests art, the abstract, imagination and order, and in "Pecksniffiana" is associated with the sky and any celestial bodies—stars, sun or moon—while "green" suggests the concrete world, nature, the wilderness, reality, chaos. This elaborate semi-private language pervades "Pecksniffiana"; most of the poems use these terms to establish some progression between the concrete and abstract worlds. In the opening poem of the group, "Fabliau of Florida," the physical world, imaged by the ocean, is joined to the sky—"Foam and cloud are one"—while in a parallel movement, the physical world of the ocean is also joined to the abstract world of the poet's imagination: "There will never be an end / To this droning of the surf." The gulf between concrete and abstract has been bridged.

The building of such a bridge is always desired and often accomplished in "Pecksniffiana." In "Ploughing on Sunday" the farmer moves from a simple and unimaginative perception of his barnyard—"The white cock's tail / Tosses in the wind / The turkey-cock's tail / Glitters in the sun"—to a musical vision of a barnyard which transcends mundane (concrete) limitations:

> Tum-ti-tum,
> Ti-tum-tum-tum!
>
> The turkey-cock's tail
> Spreads to the sun.
>
> The white cock's tail
> Streams to the moon.

In the eyes of the poet-farmer, whose imagination has become stimulated in the course of the poem, the turkeys touch earth and sky at once. Concrete and abstract are joined.

In this context of ideas and images, the poet of "Banal Sojourn" "damns that green shade at the bottom of the land," for its gross presence brings to mind the absence of

> "That bliss of stars, that princox of the evening heaven!" reminding
>   of seasons,
> When radiance came running down, slim through the bareness.

His mind, mildewing in summer, is tied to the earth, the chaotic concrete world,

> And who does not seek the sky unfuzzed, soaring to the princox?
> One has a malady, here, a malady. One feels a malady.

The malady, of course, may be traced to the poet's earthbound physical existence and conversely, to the absence of "That bliss of stars," the thought, art or truth which makes reality meaningful. Moreover, the reader of "Pecksniffiana" knows just what the patient needs, for in the second poem of "Pecksniffiana," "Homunculus et la Belle Etoile," that star, "princox of the evening heaven," "prinks" and provides the touch of abstraction which organizes the confusion of earth:

> In the sea, Biscayne, there prinks
> The young emerald, evening star,
> Good light for drunkards, poets, widows,
> And ladies soon to be married.
>
> By this light the salty fishes
> Arch in the sea like tree-branches,
> Going in many directions
> Up and down.

. . . . .

It is a good light, then, for those
That know the ultimate Plato,
Tranquillizing with this jewel
The torments of confusion.

This star, and this season of radiance, slimness, bareness is needed during the
banal sojourn of mid-summer, "swollen," "slum," "mildew," "bloated."[2] With
"this jewel" star, one can tranquillize the "torments of confusion." The poet
wishes to transcend his concrete world, to reach the sky as does the man in
"Pecksniffiana's" "Of the Surface of Things"—"The moon is in the folds of
the cloak"—and the philosopher in "Pecksniffiana's" "The Curtains in the
House of the Metaphysician," who graduates from the perception of physical
curtains to the metaphysics of the stars:

It comes about that the drifting of these curtains
Is full of long motions; as the ponderous
Deflations of distance;

. . . . .

as the firmament,
Up-rising and down-falling, bares
The last largeness, bold to see.

"Pecksniffiana" is dominated by this complex of images and attitudes:
celestial bareness is an antidote to the confusion produced by the concrete
world. Certainly "Banal Sojourn" was born of this state of mind. The poet first
demonstrates that he himself is captivated by the world of things, their number,
type, color, place: "Two wooden tubs of blue hydrangeas stand at the foot of
the stone steps." Then he cries out against the "slum of bloom," which reminds
him by contrast of "That bliss of stars" and better times, "seasons / When
radiance came running down" from the sky to earth, "slim through the
bareness." And so it is that he "damns that green shade at the bottom of the
land."

In "Banal Sojourn" Stevens mixes two metaphor patterns, summer versus
unnamed seasons, and earth versus sky, and from a distance—outside of the
original group, for instance—one might see first the less important metaphor.
Although summer is a season, and "seasons" are remembered by the narrator,

2. In the same context, the "grey and bare" jar in the Tennessee wilderness of "Anecdote of the
Jar" offers order to that chaos, but in this poem alone, of all the poems in "Pecksniffiana," the
inherent sterility of ideal solutions to the problem of chaos rises to the surface and creates a complex
and profound tone. The bare jar, as well as the wilderness, threatens us.

the poem does not describe summer as opposed to, say, winter. Instead, the poem describes the earth as opposed to the sky. The seasonal metaphor, although perhaps most obvious, is not thematically dominant; therefore neither winter nor spring is mentioned and the "seasons / When radiance came running down," times when existence was more pristine, are never imaged as times of year. The seasonal metaphor pattern is never completed—the radiant season is not imaged—because the metaphors of earth and sky take over and adequately symbolize the issues. Sukenick is not wrong in discovering a seasonal symbolism but the seasonal pattern is incomplete and subordinate to another set of images. The original group makes the exact nature of the symbolism clear: "Banal Sojourn" is a poem about phenomena threatening noumena, and phenomena and noumena are finally symbolized not by opposite seasons but by earth and sky.

"Green," then, in "Banal Sojourn" and in the rest of "Pecksniffiana" suggests an external world which is overgrown, and threatens an internal world which is undergrown. "Green" is, in this context, the enemy of the spirit.

But in the next poem of *Harmonium*, "Depression before Spring," "green" suggests the spirit itself. This total reversal of the quality and reference of an image may be most confusing in *Harmonium*, but like "Banal Sojourn," "Depression before Spring" is more accessible in the context of its original group.

"Depression before Spring" appeared a year before "Pecksniffiana" in the June, 1918, *Little Review*, in a group entitled only "Poems" which contained "Anecdote of Men by the Thousand," "Metaphors of a Magnifico," and "Depression before Spring." The group is unified by the subject of responses to the land, and by the assumption that the best response does not dramatically distort the world (as does "Pecksniffiana's" ploughman: "The white cock's tail / Streams to the moon") but simply reflects or expresses it. "Anecdote of Men by the Thousand" is about men who express their environment unconsciously ("There are men of the East . . . / Who are the East"), and "Metaphors of a Magnifico" is about a man who cannot express either his environment or himself at all. He tries to describe a simple scene, of "Twenty men crossing a bridge, / Into a village," and becomes so confused with the metaphysics of the scene, with twenty bridges and twenty villages or one man and one village, that he fails to find words sufficient to the task:

> That will not declare itself
> Yet is certain as meaning . . .

Finally, unable to steady his mind with a naming of objects, he loses entirely his hold on the scene and on himself:

> The first white wall of the village
> Rises through fruit-trees.
> Of what was I thinking?
> So the meaning escapes.

> The first wall of the village . . .
> The fruit trees. . . .

That is the end of the poem. The poet—the "Magnifico" of metaphors—is at a loss for words, and cannot respond to the natural scene with an accurate description. He is not like the men and women of the first poem of the group, "Anecdote of Men by the Thousand," who are in harmony with their environment:

> The soul, he said, is composed
> Of the external world.
> There are men of the East, he said,
> Who are the East.
>
> .   .   .   .   .
>
> The dress of a woman of Lhassa,
> In its place,
> Is an invisible element of that place
> Made visible.

Neither as poet nor as native is the "Magnifico" part of a place; he cannot even describe its action.

"Depression before Spring" is the third poem of the group, following a poem about harmony with one's environment ("There are men of the East . . . / Who are the East") and a poem about discord between a "Magnifico" poet and his environment. "Depression before Spring" is also about a man's separation from his environment and the ensuing incompetence of his expression. Like "Metaphors of a Magnifico," the poem is narrated by a bad poet. This origin explains the problematic second stanza, which is a curious exhibition of the narrator's poetic poverty:

> The cock crows
> But no queen rises.
>
> The hair of my blonde
> Is dazzling,
> As the spittle of cows
> Threading the wind.
>
> Ho! Ho!
>
> But ki-ki-ri-ki
> Brings no rou-cou.
> No rou-cou-cou.

> But no queen comes
> In slipper green.

Spring, in the form of a cock, calls "ki-ki-ri-ki," but within the poet no corresponding fertility, no queen, no "rou-cou-cou" rises. As proof of his depressing sterility, the narrator offers in the second stanza an example of his poetry—a magnifico's metaphor, a buffoon's fling at courtly flattery in which his lover's hair is compared to cow spit. "Ho! Ho!" is either an appropriately weak continuation of his lyric or a sarcastic comment on it. Since the visually perfect but gauche image of cow spit reflects a strangely mechanical and unsymphathetic response to a woman, the reader has a choice of taste; he may consider the stanza itself ridiculous, or he may consider it an apt image of a poor response to spring-time stimuli. Either way the poet has failed. His imagination is inadequate.

The genre in which the poet fails is, of course, love poetry, for if spring comes, sex will not be far behind: the queen is at once a hen for the rooster, the blonde whom he cannot gracefully image, and almost anything fertile—the imagination, a good poem. The numerous sexual images and allusions are broadened by the second stanza, which extends the concept of impotence to poetry, and by the final "green," which suggests that the answering "rou-cou-cou" would not be sexual alone, but a general, spring-like, vitality. The vitality in question would be inside the narrating poet; exactly when the cock crows in the calendar year is not important, for it is the poet's imagination which has yet to thaw or blossom or strut. The winter could last for years.

Thus the seasonal symbolism of this poem, too, is more complex than one might suppose. The "Spring" of the title, and the "green" at the end, symbolize imaginative fertility, and so the opposite of "spring" in this poem is not imaged by winter, but by inadequate poetry: "The hair of my blonde / Is dazzling / As the spittle of cows / Threading the wind." The poet is depressed by his incompetence. In musical terms—which are to Stevens poetic terms—the poet cannot sing "Tum-ti-tum" as did the ploughman of "Pecksniffiana's" "Ploughing on Sunday"; he has no musical response: "But ki-ki-ri-ki / Brings no rou-cou. . . . "

This group of three poems is unified by a very different atmosphere from that of "Pecksniffiana," for it is not filled with a threatening physical world. Even the jungles of "Metaphors of a Magnifico," which might well have appeared as a "slum of bloom," remain dry and distant; the subject is not natural growth during a banal sojourn, but human reticence. Similarly, "Anecdote of Men by the Thousand" does not take advantage of its exotic elements: it mentions the East and Lhassa in business-like fashion, to illustrate the blend of some people with their places. Since the physical world is not threatening in this group, there is none of the emotional reaction to "green" found in "Banal Sojourn." The "Depression before Spring" group is less intense than "Pecksniffiana," and concerned not with overwhelming fecundity but with sterility. In the mental desert of the Magnifico's metaphors and the poet's depression some inner vitality—a queen in slipper green—is needed.

The *Harmonium* companions "Banal Sojourn" and "Depression before Spring" come from different worlds; the poet is threatened in one world by fecundity outside—the rotting summer growth—and in the other, by sterility within. Both of the original groups are internally consistent and self-explicative. The poet of "Depression before Spring" wishes his soul, like that of the woman of Lhassa in "Anecdote of Men by the Thousand," to be "composed of the external world." Then a "Ki-ki-ri-ki" will bring a "rou-cou-cou" from the poet. But he can respond to his external world neither with native natural harmony (there are men of the barnyard who are the barnyard), nor with the touring poet's harmony of appropriate metaphor. The poet of "Banal Sojourn," on the other hand, finds himself too much composed of the external world, and under the threat of physical surfeit his spiritual hope is best imaged by slim, bare radiance, opposites of "green." Rather than be composed of his external world, he would compose—in the sense of order—it. Thus the bare, alien jar dominating the wilderness in "Pecksniffiana's" "Anecdote of the Jar" is the exact opposite of "an invisible element of that place / Made visible" ("Anecdote of Men by the Thousand").

The juxtaposition of "Banal Sojourn" and "Depression before Spring" in *Harmonium* produces intriguing if confusing contrasts. We cannot accept the two greens only as identical images of natural growth, which is anticipated before spring and hated in summer. Yet in both cases "green" suggests vitality. Paradoxically, when we recognize that "green" represents in "Banal Sojourn" a threatening external vitality, and in "Depression before Spring" a cherished internal vitality, we find that the poems come together as expressions of mental malaise, a malaise which strikes once in "Depression before Spring" when the poet doesn't respond to the physical world and again in "Banal Sojourn" when he doesn't resist it. These two poems reflect the ambivalence of Stevens' approach to nature. After 1917, he was repeatedly attracted to a physical world which was potentially loathsome—"our old bane, green and bloated." His love and fear of the physical is perfectly represented by the parent groups of these two poems: should we be composed of the external world, or should we compose it? Is harmony natural or artificial? The difficulty of *Harmonium* lies in the intersection of these two attitudes at the single word "green," although reference to the original groups helps indicate the directions of both poems and the contrasts dramatized by their common image.

Stevens, in juxtaposing these two poems, did not invite the reader to share with him a single symbolic structure built of many pieces, or a single mood or point of view or even subject developed in different ways—all of which he shared with readers in his original groups and in stanzaic poems such as "Thirteen Ways of Looking at a Blackbird"; instead, he suddenly, in 1923, called new attention to each poem, forced us to look, and look again. Yet as he invited such "contextual" criticism, he also thwarted it. In removing poems from congenial and sympathetic companions, Stevens deprived readers of the

countless keys, forged by inter-poem associations, which unlock private symbols; in extreme cases, he gave us the wrong key—such as one type of response
to "green"—and invited us to try the lock of an adjoining poem.

Why did Stevens in 1922 strike a new pose, making his poems more obscure
and complicating his relation to his readers, and what happened to the old
groups, to their continuity and homogeneity? Within the limits of this essay
I cannot discuss Stevens' development during the *Harmonium* period; instead,
I will describe briefly the relationship of the original groups to *Harmonium* and
how *Harmonium* was assembled; then I will try to suggest why an arrangement
based on contrasts pleased Stevens in 1922 and how that arrangement affects
our reading.

The original groups of the period 1914 to 1923 did not suffer random
damage; they were systematically dispersed in *Harmonium.* Of the fifty-three
group poems in *Harmonium,* only two have their original companions,[3] and
only four others are next to any poems from their original groups.[4] Merely
dating the poems of *Harmonium* reveals one source of contrast, for Stevens
changed from 1914 to 1923 and poems from different years tended to be
different in certain ways. If the dates of first publication of the first eight poems,
for instance, are written into the *Harmonium* table of contents, the shuffling
of dates is apparent: 1918, 1921, 1917, 1919, 1917, 1921, 1916, 1921. Furthermore, by writing the group of origin beside the date of each poem in
Harmonium, we see that groups were usually shuffled even when dates were
not. For instance, two poems from 1918 are adjacent ("Nuances of a Theme
by Williams" and "Metaphors of a Magnifico," *CP,* 18-19); originally, the
poems were in different groups, both published in 1918, and the groups had
different characters. Thus *Harmonium* covered Stevens' tracks. His development
from 1914 to 1923, which has not been noted by critics, was hidden by his
mixing of dates. The original groups disappeared.

Where the groups went is best illustrated by a short history of "Phases,"
a history which also reveals how Stevens' treatment of groups is curiously
parallel to his treatment of some single poems and reflects a peculiar inconfidence about the integrity of his pieces. From "Phases" (1914), a highly integrat-
ed group of four poems on a war theme, he plucked the fourth poem—IV—or
perhaps we should call it the fourth section, titled it "In Battle" and allowed
it to be anthologized in *The New Poetry* of 1917. He never reunited the four
poems, or the four sections of a single poem, of the original group, and he did
not include them in his books. When we remember how Stevens allowed
"Sunday Morning" in its first printing to be cut and rearranged by Harriet

3. "On the Manner of Addressing Clouds" and "Of Heaven Considered as a Tomb," both *CP,*
55, and originally printed adjacent in the group "Sur Ma Guzzla Gracile," 1921.

4. "The Place of the Solitaires," "The Weeping Burgher," "The Curtains in the House of the
Metaphysician" and "Banal Sojourn," *CP,* 60-62, are all from "Pecksniffiana," but were originally
in a different order. It is interesting to note that "The Curtains in the House of the Metaphysician"
and "The Place of the Solitaires" were adjacent in the group and formed a nice pair, as Stevens
attests in his letters (*L,* 463-64), but were separated in *Harmonium.*

Monroe, we realize that to Stevens the integrity of poems and groups was very loose, and the longest inviolable unit was often the section or stanza. Thus the sections of "Sunday Morning" must have been to Stevens very much like separate poems on a single theme gathered in one group. To Miss Monroe he said only:

> Provided your selection of the numbers of "Sunday Morning" is printed in the following order: I, VIII, IV, V, I see no objection to cutting it down. The order is necessary to the idea.
>
> •   •   •   •   •
>
> No. 7 of "Sunday Morning" is, as you suggest, of a different tone, but it does not seem to me too detached to conclude with. (*L,* 183)

Stevens' curious treatment of "Phases" and "Sunday Morning" raises a perplexing question: what are the boundaries of a Stevens poem? Is "Sunday Morning" a group of several poems? Most critics would consider it whole and complete only as it is now printed in *Collected Poems,* but Stevens at one time apparently did not agree. Conversely, are some of the poems from groups not poems at all but fragments? "Phases" I-IV, I would say, is a single poem, and in that case Stevens erred in tearing a fragment loose and titling it. A poem such as "Banal Sojourn" or "Depression before Spring" may be so dependent on original group associations that its integrity as a work of art is in question. Although the individual poems of *Harmonium* are, I think, complete, they are also distressingly dependent on private systems of symbols and associations. Even if no poems in *Harmonium* are absolutely unintelligible as they stand, there are many which, severed from their original groups and arranged as they are in *Harmonium,* become extremely obscure. Such obscurity may well have been the intentional result of Stevens' inconfidence, which, as we shall see, was remarkable in 1922.

Few of the groups which Stevens dispersed have been reunited, so that critics must scramble to gain an alternative view of the *Harmonium* period. Although the four sections of "Phases," for instance, appear in the *Opus Posthumous,* Samuel French Morse has also added two more manuscript "Phases" and numbered them V and VI, thus destroying the sequence which the original group offered. Even this degree of restoration is rare. Some of the poems of "Pecksniffiana" were anthologized together between 1919 and 1923, and the entire group was reprinted in *Prize Poems* of 1930, but that was the last printing of the group. Its poems are spread through *Harmonium* and the *Opus Posthumous.* The early work of Stevens is still known almost exclusively by the book he created in 1922.

What sort of book was it? From 1914 to 1923 Stevens published almost 120 poems, and from these he chose sixty-six for *Harmonium.* He included in the first edition of his book only seven poems which had not been published elsewhere. The 1923 *Harmonium* was therefore not a first book of new poems. It was rather a first collected poems, made mostly of old material previously published in magazines. Three-fourths of its poems, moreover, had been collected before in groups and these early collections had placed the poems in a context of homogeneity, very different from the heterogeneity of *Harmonium*. Stevens' tendency to fragment, divide, section, split up into isolated entities, a tendency which dominated many of his stanzaic poems and his treatment of "Sunday Morning," seems to have reached a peak in his ordering, or disordering of *Harmonium*. This desire to fragment is accurately reflected in the title he once preferred for his book, *The Grand Poem: Preliminary Minutiae*.

Within *Harmonium*, each poem of the period stands in intriguing isolation. The contrasting uses of "green" in "Banal Sojourn" and "Depression before Spring" are unusually mechanical, but almost all the poems are in pleasing if less violent conflict with their neighbors. For instance, most of the poems mentioned in this essay have strange companions. In a parallel to the contrast of "Pecksniffiana's" "Banal Sojourn" and "Depression before Spring," "Pecksniffiana's" "Ploughing on Sunday" was placed next to another poem of the "Depression before Spring" group, "Metaphors of a Magnifico"; this pair forms a contrast of articulate and reticent narrations. In assembling the book Stevens repeatedly juxtaposed poems from groups of exceptionally conflicting character; many of the "Pecksniffiana" poems (1919) were placed next to those of another large group, "Sur Ma Guzzla Gracile" (1921), which differed from "Pecksniffiana" in distinctive ways. "Homunculus et la Belle Etoile" from "Pecksniffiana" was placed next to a poem from "Sur Ma Guzzla Gracile" ("Another Weeping Woman"), as was "Anecdote of the Jar" (next to "Palace of the Babies"). Throughout *Harmonium*, the mixing of dissimilar groups and the juxtaposition of dissimilar poems is so common that it appears methodical.

Certainly Stevens must have revelled in such contrasts. They confuse, tickle, tease, complicate and obscure, and those would seem to be the very effects he sought in 1922, for he was not impressed with his "old" poems and he feared that his book would be dull:

> Gathering together the things for my book has been so depressing that I wonder at *Poetry's* friendliness. All my earlier things seem like horrid cocoons from which later abortive insects have sprung. The book will amount to nothing except that it may teach me something. . . . Only, the reading of these outmoded and debilitated poems does make me wish rather desperately to keep on dabbling and to be as obscure as possible until I have invented an authentic and fluent speech for myself. (*L*, 231)

Thus he assembled *Harmonium*, apparently, on the principle which guided his second book, *Ideas of Order*. To prevent a "colorless" tone in *Ideas of Order*, he prescribed some new poems and "an arrangement . . . simply based on contrasts":

> After I had made a tentative arrangement of the material, it seemed to me that the tone of the whole might be a bit low and colorless; and, since it

is the tone of the whole that is important, I might want to work on the thing, adding, say, ten or fifteen pages, in order to give a little gaiety and brightness. My mind is not ordinarily as lamentable as some of these poems suggest. (1934, *L*, 272-3)

On the whole, the result is rather decent, I think. The more recent poems have been spread more or less through the manuscript. The arrangement is simply based on contrasts; there is nothing rigid about it. (1935, *L*, 279)

Stevens varied the pace of *Harmonium* as much as possible by utilizing contrasts: he mixed his newer poems with the "outmoded" ones and dispersed the old homogeneous groups. He used contrasts to make what he considered dull and "debilitated" poetry less obvious and monotonous, yet actually he was pushing his poems further in the very direction he had been travelling—toward shock, novelty, contrast, exoticism. In 1922, as he assembled the book, he was also writing and publishing his most exotic poetry: "Bantams in Pine-Woods," "A High-Toned Old Christian Woman," "The Comedian as the Letter C," "Frogs Eat Butterflies. Snakes Eat Frogs. Hogs Eat Snakes. Men Eat Hogs" and "The Emperor of Ice Cream." At no other period of his life did he take more delight in ironic contrasts, in "flowers in last month's newspapers." *Harmonium* was assembled during an important year of Stevens' development, at a time when contrast had become not just a device, but a primary virtue.

The arrangement of *Harmonium* is therefore aesthetically functional. In arranging his book Stevens sought what he had begun to seek in all his poetry: through imaginative distortions, to turn the world to better account. *Harmonium*, then, marks in a curious way Stevens' coming of age. It is not that all the poems of *Harmonium* are dominated by his mature aesthetic, by dramatically contrasting elements held in tension by verse, but that all—even early and rather more straightforward poems—are so arranged as to increase the tensions he had come to admire. The contrasts of *Harmonium* and the difficulties that arise from the arrangement of the book, like the contrasts and difficulties within many poems, are part of the distortion and artifice, the wrenching and twisting, the perverting that for the mature Stevens both mirrors the human condition and gives delight:

> The imperfect is our paradise.
> Note that, in this bitterness, delight,
> Since the imperfect is so hot in us,
> Lies in flawed words and stubborn sounds.
> ("The Poems of Our Climate," 1938)

This arrangement of the book has had several effects on our understanding of Stevens: his early development has remained hidden, and many poems have remained enigmatic because they are more difficult when separated from their original groups; but more generally, the arrangement of the book has led to an exaggeration of the role of contrast in Stevens' work, has bolstered his reputation as "the great Dandy of American Letters,"[5] "Dandy, Eccentric, Clown."[6] In *Harmonium,* the reader's attention is diverted from any continuity in Stevens' thought or development and is focused on contrasting fragments of a kaleidoscopic vision; in so arranging the book, Stevens emphasized the brilliance and autonomy of each piece, but he also made himself appear more eccentric and whimsical than he was, or rather, had been. Paradoxically, this exaggeration of the role of contrast in Stevens' early poetry has occurred precisely because we have *not* seen that the arrangement itself generates contrasts; consequently, a general tone or atmosphere of eccentricity, partially created by the arrangement of the poems, is attributed solely to oddities within the poems themselves.

The arrangement of *Harmonium* may have proved deceptive, but it is not unfortunate. Although it has slowed scholarship by misrepresenting the early Stevens and by obscuring many poems, the contrived arrangement, when recognized, brings many buried poems to life and is itself yet another artifice which, through "flawed words and stubborn sounds," gives delight.

From *English Literary History,* 37 (1970), 456-73.

5. M. L. Rosenthal, *The Modern Poets* (New York: Oxford University Press, 1965), p. 131.

6. A chapter title in Robert Buttel's *Wallace Stevens, The Making of Harmonium* (Princeton: Princeton University Press, 1967).

EDWARD GUERESCHI

"The Comedian as the Letter C": Stevens' Anti-Mythological Poem

I

RECENT CRITICISM on Wallace Stevens' poetry tends to regard *Owl's Clover* as the outstanding example of a radical shift in Stevens' viewpoint. Louis L. Martz comments that in this poem Stevens gave up his belief in the earthly apotheosis of mankind for an almost bitter and stringent view of how deformed man appears "in a place / That is not our own." But it has not been noticed that Stevens, thirteen years earlier in *Harmonium* (1923), had already undercut the idea of a marriage of "flesh and air." When his poetry was translated into Italian (*Mattino Domincale,* tr. Renato Poggioli), Stevens spoke of the "Comedian's" "anti-mythological" purpose, expressed by the conventional adventures of an "every-day man" who lives in a "poetic atmosphere, as we all do." This statement, unusually direct for a man who wrote even his essays as if they were poems, asserts Stevens' early wish to describe reality as-it-is, without the romantic trappings of myth. Viewed from the enlightened perspective of his complete work, the "Comedian" dramatizes more successfully than *Owl's Clover* the struggle to envision a reality of the "quotidian." The "quotidian" is the poet's value term for suggesting the continuously pressing "violence" of commonplace reality experienced without the false panacea of myth. To establish his bold assumption that the apotheosis of man is not enough, Stevens chose to write a mock-heroic satire on the archetypal symbol of American self-confidence and assertiveness—the figure of Adam.

Stevens' ambitious satire is directed against the venerated myth of the American Adam. His quarrel with Adam involves an emphatic denial of the naive folklore and transcendental optimism which formulizes the myth. As envisioned by Emerson and Whitman and interpreted by R. W. B. Lewis, the Adamic myth foresaw:

> an individual emancipated from history, happily bereft of ancestry, untouched and undefiled by the usual Inheritances of Family and race; an individual standing alone; self-reliant and self-propelling; ready to confront whatever awaited him with the aid of his own unique and inherent resources.

In addition to characterizing Adam with his attitude of stalwart independence from nature and mundane circumstance, the myth's poetic and psychological efficacy unrealistically gives credence, in Richard Chase's words, to "these crises of life by an appeal to the past, to the traditions of culture, or to the superhuman powers of heroes." Such transfigurations, however, did not impress Stevens, who believed that "the ultimate value is reality," and for whom a mythological construct remained as defunct as (his own analogy) Plato's winged charioteer. In Stevens' poetry, particularly "The Comedian as the Letter C," the resulting shift in values focuses attention upon man's unheroic behavior in an unheroic age. His hero is the clown, pathetic and contradictory, the logical representative of an age of anxiety, and his poem is the ironic documentary of an unsupported mythology in which the mighty Adam is shrunken to the clown Crispin.

The dramatic qualities of the American myth are elaborarately burlesqued in the poem's racy, impertinent familiarity with the once-sacred. As Constance Rourke has observed, "mythologies do not lend themselves to small or delicate comic intricacies." Stevens exposes the numerous stereotypes underlying the Adamic formula by mock-heroic reversals that parody Crispin's magnified aspirations. The unlimited horizon from which Adam drew breathing-space is considerably reduced to a deprecatory "simple salad-beds" overlooking a "nice shady home." Crispin's new-born innocence (like Adam's) is comically fleeced by the shell-game tricks of the naturalistic world. Even the arrogant claim of stoical independence (that old cry of Thoreau's) is comically domesticated by "four daughters with curls." Contraction follows expansion throughout Crispin's disillusioning adventures. Mockingly described as the "Socrates of snails," he ludicrously confronts the unknown terrors once assigned to the Promethean heroes of *Moby Dick* and *Leatherstocking*. The redemptive qualities of nature (the wilderness of Cooper and Faulkner) are metamorphosed into the pleasure-spas of Yucatan and Havana. And in a sardonic denial of traditional spiritual and poetic values, Triton, romantic custodian of the waters, is drowned by the unlucky event of having outlived his legendary age. Simultaneously, the musical analogies dotted throughout appear to mock the affirmative lyricism of the bardic "Song of Myself" in a "polyphony beyond Crispin's thrust." His "pipping sounds" furnish an ironic incongruity with the "hallucinating horn" that sang before of man's security in the divine "kosmos."

Critics have noted that Crispin serves experience like a valet, and even displays some of the wise cunning of the archetypal Arlecchino or Figaro. But it seems more consistent with Stevens' advice to view him as the dupe of Christian idealism, a seeker after truth in an age where traditional values have become an anachronism. Appropriately enough, his namesake is St. Crispin, the third-century patron saint of shoemakers. Like his distant yet kindred ancestor, Crispin undergoes extreme (but useless) hardships for the sake of his illusions. St. Crispin mockingly referred to himself as the "Capuchin ass," a phrase which Stevens echoes and irreverently modernizes in a satire of his hero's noble aspirations. "What was the purpose of his pilgrimage . . . if not . . . To make a new intelligence prevail?" As the seeker after truth, Crispin represents the naive terminal view of Emersonian idealism with "Nature" as its sacred text: "man is conscious of a universal soul within or behind his individual life, wherein, as in a firmament, the natures of Justice, Truth, Love, Freedom arise and shine." Embracing these Platonic abstractions, Crispin sadly discovers that "the plum survives its poems"; absolute truth, even if in the guise of poetry, cannot transcend reality, if reality is to remain more than an illusion. The failure of a mythopoeic rebirth ("green brag") and the subsequent acceptance of the "quotidian" or commonplace facts of reality is sardonically announced in the concluding line—"So may the relation of each man be clipped." Eventually, all men are "clipped" of their fondest illusions and assume the reluctant responsibilities of what they have sown. For Crispin it is as it began: a rueful commitment to the mundane.

The mock-heroic elements furnish a comic series of deadpan attitudes and sudden reversals (all of which are suitable for a clown); but they do not disguise the poet's skeptical reservations of a transcendental vision. Santayana, a close source for Stevens' thought, also clipped the wings of idealists:

Mind was not created for the sake of discovering the absolute truth. The absolute truth has its own intangible reality and scorns to be known. The function of mind is rather to increase the wealth of the universe in the spiritual dimension, by adding appearance to substance and passion to ecstasy, and by creating all those *private* perspectives and those emotions of wonder, adventure, curiosity and laughter which omniscience would exclude.

The philosopher's hedonistic compromise with the world's body finds a sympathetic parallel in "The Comedian as the Letter C." The private and comic sensibility, opposed to the public and heroic posture, furnishes the theme's tension. The latter designates a false and hollow domination over nature, expressed by the poetic proposition: "Man is the intelligence of his soil." The former unites man to his world without the benefit of myth: "His soil is man's intelligence." The dualism is tested and refined by the impassive "quotidian" which resists Crispin's efforts of transcendence. For Stevens, the "quotidian" also represents deterministic fate, an impenetrable power hostile to the illusions of mythology. Such is the force that snickers at Crispin's vain aspirations for immortality:

> the quotidian
> Like this, saps like the sun, true fortuner.
> For all it takes it gives a humped return
> Exchequering from piebald fiscs unkeyed.

Less generally, Stevens' line of resistance to the mythological can be traced in three stages applicable to corresponding sections of the poem: the denial of man's herioc destiny (I, II); the difficulties of apotheosizing Eden (II, III, IV); and the failure of the mythopoeic imagination (V, VI).

II

The denial of man's heroic destiny. The heroic image of Walt Whitman's "Passage to India" is the confident figure of Adam, or Man Seeing, triumphantly journeying toward his manifest destiny. In his poem, Whitman praises the "infinite glories of the past" and optimistically connects its beginnings to the future. Fifty-five years later, Stevens severs Whitman's coaxial cable by bluntly rejecting the antiquated forms that contribute to the disorder of reality. By acknowledging the naturalism that is inherent in reality, Stevens can dispel the hoary patterns of nobility, heroism, and magniloquence from today's calendar. In his essay, "The Noble Rider and the Sound of Words," Stevens writes with the awareness that "the dump is full of images":

> It is hard to think of a thing more out of time than nobility. Looked at plainly it seems false and dead and ugly. To look at it at all makes us realize sharply that in our present, in the presence of reality, the past looks false, and is, therefore, dead, and is therefore, ugly; and we turn away from the characteristic that it has a way of assuming; something that was noble in its day, grandeur that was, the rhetorical once.

The transition from a "grandeur that was" to Crispin's naturalistic world is made by peeling away the falsely sentimental preconceptions which incrust "reality." Tradition created its heroes by boldly asserting man's will against the hazards of nature (Whitman's vision of "man against the open sky"). And similarly, the archetypal images of the sea and thunderstorm (which dominate the opening sections of the "Comedian"), once were exploited as romantic props to illustrate man's spiritual victory over nature. Yet reality resists such hyperbole, Stevens believes, because its abstract forms outlast the temporal assumptions of speculative thought. Each age creates its own artifacts which in turn give birth to their own versions of reality. What occurs when these traditional artifacts no longer compel belief is the problem of "The World without Imagination."

"What counted was mythology of self, / Blotched out beyond unblotching." To erase Crispin's narcissism demands an act of nature sufficiently arresting to overwhelm his dated preconceptions. As the "nincompated pedagogue," Crispin pedantically rules over his environment, yet his supercilious arrogance prohibits a successful identification with the "simple salad-beds" that nurtured him. Consequently, his epithet is suitably effete; with a "barber's eye," he can smugly if inaccurately contain his rendition of nature within a curl or coiffure. But comically, his hair's-breadth view of reality is split by a confrontation with the terrible neutrality of the sea. Revealing himself to be actually "A skinny sailor peering in the sea-glass," the lover of "maidenly greenhorns" is "washed away by magnitude." Inevitably, the poses of the romantic self must succumb before the evident reality of a hostile nature. And Crispin's ludicrous self-estimations furnish an ironic aside on the affected attitudes toward nature that existed in the nineteenth century ("that century of wind"). In Wordsworth's

"The world is too much with us; late and soon," a sonnet that nearly reverses
the circumstances in the "Comedian," the image of the sea is transformed by
the poet into an object of melancholy desire. Initially, the sea possesses the
fascination of a temptress who "bares her bosom to the moon"; finally it
becomes a metaphor to express Wordsworth's hunger for antiquity, and his
wish to again "hear old Triton blow his wreathed horn." By contrast, Stevens'
chill sea is the bottomless depository for those accumulated, outmoded concepts
that swam through romantic waters. And Triton, no longer a symbol for the
allure of heroic ages, exists only in "faint, memorial gesturing." His epic
adventures, once hymned by Vergil, are now forgotten by the radical skepticism
of a later age. The romantic prototypes, which no longer retain their efficacy
before reality, create a dramatic metaphor of alienation that states Crispin's
unimaginative view of the universe. For to possess an imagination is to inte-
grate the self with the world so that no obstruction (romantic or otherwise)
will destroy belief. Finally aware of the necessity of remodeling his views,
"Crispin beheld and Crispin was made new."

The combination of circumstances which eventually resigns the "poetic
hero" to his fate is heavily accented with ironic reservations. His quest, unlike
that of the self-assured figures of romance, never ends in a revelation that
dwarfs the surrounding world. Instead, he is made aware of a naturalistic truth,
that the restrictions environment imposes upon man ironically provide just
enough freedom to comprehend the nature of those limitations. This anti-
transcendental view is the basis for Crispin's loss of egoism before unconcerned
reality. Such is the lesson learned at Yucatan, where the newly discovered
liberty to conceive of reality must bow to the sobering restrictions of man's
environment, the domination of the "soil." For Crispin, this discovery remains
as annihilating as the knowledge brought from the sea. It proclaims something
"harsher than he learned / From hearing signboards whimper in cold nights."
Simply, the thunderstorm over Yucatan announces his bondage to nature and
the discovery of his insignificant humanity:

> He knelt in the cathedral with the rest,
> This connoisseur of elemental fate,
> Aware of exquisite thought.

Diminished to an initial, to his essential self, Crispin's effacement denies the
Adamic principle of "freedom through knowledge" conspicuously woven in the
fabric of the American myth and which proclaims man's transcendence over
nature. By forsaking the illusion of conquest, Crispin discovers that the naturalistic paradox of freedom-through-bondage brings him closer to the poetic
reality he wishes to "vociferate" departing for America.

> His mind was free
> And more than free, elate, intent, profound
> And studious of a self possessing him,

That was not in him in the crusty town
From which he sailed.

III

The difficulty of apotheosizing Eden. "To give a sense of the freshness of a world" is, of course, a central concern for *Harmonium*. What Crispin has discovered is for Stevens, a fundamental truth; that identity and fulfillment must derive from sensual reality. In this way, Stevens' "theme of delight" appears to be the twentieth-century extension of Whitman's myth of Eden which unites the world with paradise. But the same restrictions that bow Crispin to his fate also make Stevens view his world more realistically. As the "inquisitorial botanist" romantically chants of the "kosmos," he surprisingly discovers that the role of plebeian and realist leaves little room for discriminating between the real and what is actually desired of it. That is, without the necessary refinements of the imagination, the world is nothing more than chaotic. Nature's "spirits" come "so thick with sides of jagged lops of green . . . so like a jostling festival," that in distaste, Crispin finds refuge in the patrician role of "annotator." Bruised yet adamant, he approaches Carolina (III), pondering over the lessons of his "heroic" journey.

He now "conceived his voyaging to be / An up and down between two elements, / A fluctuating between sun and moon." Crispin's dilemma (it is also Stevens') is a matter of aesthetic refinement. To create poetry in bardic fashion, in the name of sensual reality, is to deny order and discrimination for disorder and equalitarianism. Conversely, the romantic imagination suggests only a peripheral contact with the world, distorting what is real for what is preferred to be real by the imagination. However, by treating these opposing forces in terms of sun and moon, Stevens infers their natural impingement upon each other. Solely by the interaction between imagination and reality can there be created a satisfactory view of existence. Crispin's skeptical reservations on the imagination's behavior derive from a sad experience of failure ("America was always north to him"), because he had envisioned his homeland in terms of romantic myth. Now to exchange unromantic "quotidian" reality for earlier transcendental hopes may herald the end of his Adamic vision of the New World.

Meekly, "without palms / Or jugglery," Crispin enters a back seaport of Carolina. But his western voyage ends in sunlight. The "moonlight fiction" vanished and he "savored rankness like a sensualist." The journey which began with intimations of immortality is ingloriously completed with the smell of "rancid rosin" and the view of "marshy ground." Yet Crispin is pleased because he discovers that aesthetic satisfactions, even though expressed in disenchantment, nonetheless require the imagination's aid and make possible the synthesis that creates poetry.

He gripped more closely the essential prose

As being, in a world so falsified,
The one integrity for him, the one
Discovery still possible to make,
To which all poems were incident, unless
That prose should wear a poem's guise at last.

With the syllables of the sea and thunderstorm, the "essential prose" shares a firm belief in the commonplace. At first, the "quotidian" as prose, appears to resist imaginative perception, until it becomes evident that the commonplace depends upon its elevating power for expression. Consequently, the perceptions which discover rich value in the ordinary world are the poetic expressions that define the world. Thus prose becomes poetry merely by the act of perceiving the "quotidian" of everyday reality. In his new Eden, Crispin's desire is to apotheosize this synthesis of the imaginative with the mundane.

His education in the ways of the world ends with the knowledge that the "soil is man's intelligence." Like everything else learned on his voyage, this awareness is ambiguously enlightening and restrictive. To recognize the paternity of the "soil" is to find joy in discovering a unity between humanity and nature: "the natives of the rain are rainy men." But, alternatively, such a union poses the aesthetic problem of perceiving the appropriate poetry which will not falsify reality. Sardonically, Stevens comments on Crispin's search for a reality that will celebrate Eden:

What Eden sapling gum, what honeyed gore,
What pulpy dram distilled of innocence,
That streaking gold should speak in him
Or bask within his images and words?

But to envision a new Eden is to create a new order in reality. Like Stevens' well-known jar that subjugated the Tennessee wilderness to its form, Crispin likewise attempts to create an order that will sustain an aesthetic vision over nature. Yet he fails to realize that in the metamorphosis both the creator and creation are altered by a new identification "Like nothing else in Tennessee." As arch-realist, Crispin could not accept such a transformation of self. Instead, he chooses to imitate the process of nature without the artifacts of a "blundering" design.

Although Crispin becomes an evangelist for the new gospel of the "quotidian," his knowledge of reality is distorted by the same romantic idealism that mythicized Whitman's vision of "democratic vistas." Like Whitman, he fails to comprehend that to reproduce nature is actually to reinterpret it. His first "central hymns" promulgate the "miracles" to be performed in the New World, with the "florist asking aid from cabbages" and the "blind man" comically playing the role of "astronomer." With the added emphasis of ritual and ceremony, his apotheosis would result in a mimetic act, a sterile counterfeit of roles copied from nature. Inevitably, Crispin's rosy Eden would become an "art-for-art's-sake" school, an esoteric purification of "quotidian" reality. Apotheosis, Crispin sadly realizes, is another mythopoeic act that filches from the real to create the ideal; for this reason, the "progenitor of such extensive scope" could not be content with resurrecting old forms under new masks. Humiliated, he undertakes the role of clown, serving "grotesque apprenticeship to chance event."

The clown-figure, which is pivotal to Stevens' comedy, has caused a good deal of speculation. Dramatically antithetical to the Promethean hero, the clown exists not in the center of events, but on their periphery, wisely acknowledging the incomprehensibility of reality. Neither quite like Eliot's "Prufrock" or Yeat's "Fool," his buffoon-humanity suggests the pathos of Chaplin's clown, over-anxious to emulate heroes, yet, in his inevitable fall, able to make some reconciliation with the world. Both Chaplin and Stevens find their closest images of the clown in Greek legend: Chaplin in the image of Pan, and Stevens, probably in the figure of Silenus, the satyr-god of comedy, who is known as the "wise fool" who acknowledges the irreconcilables in existence. Like Silenus, Crispin the clown admits to a sad incompatibility; his romantic predilections will forever betray his attempts to determine the ultimate nature of reality. Such sophisticated disillusionment, however, provokes a certain degree of self-knowledge. Shrewdly, Crispin forsakes his synthetic role of seer by substituting for the mystic's epiphany chance insights that attend the appearance of things. He has discovered the psychological truth that introspection distorts the world-as-it-is, coloring it with the self's own desires and frustrations.

As to Crispin's former dreams of Eden, Stevens tartly retorts: "All dreams are vexing. Let them be expunged."

IV

The failure of the mythopoeic imagination. All the defects hostile to heroes but undeniable for clowns converge upon Crispin in the concluding, coda-like sections of the "Comedian." His masculine world (in which sexual abstinence is a prime requirement for mythic heroes) yields to domesticity, complacency, and fatalism. In this comically naturalistic manner, the challenger of the cosmos pays retribution to the commonplace for once denying its efficacy. Bound by his own moral principle: "For realist, is is what should be," Crispin can do little except swallow and await his fate, a life of bourgeois conventionality. As "The blue infected will," draining away ambitions of colony-building, Crispin becomes comfortably aware of the narrow yet satisfying attractions of his environment. Relinquishing dreams of apotheosizing Eden in verse, he admits that "The words of things entangle and confuse. The plum survives its poems." Love swiftly follows serenity, and soon, in a "nice shady home," rest Crispin, his "duenna" and "four daughters with curls."

However, such domestic entanglements are not performed without regret for former days spent in the pursuit of Elysium. In fact, Crispin as Babbitt is rescued from dull mediocrity by a nettling sight: his lost dreams come reproduced "in purple" by his progeny. Since they are direct products of Crispin the man, they comically reflect attitudes of Crispin the erstwhile Adamic poet.

In the order of their birth, they hilariously signify a renaissance of forgotten arts: music, by the "vermeil capuchin" who satirically gives "the dulcet omen fit for such a house"; passion, by the second daughter, who is a "hot embosomer"; prosody, by a "pearly poetess, peaked for rhapsody"; inspiration, by "the fourth, pent now, a digit curious." In sum, they characterize "the same insoluble lump" by which Crispin had identified the world. Comically, this four-part invention forms a string quartet (played on the key of "C" with Crispin anxiously conducting) that mockingly identifies the *paterfamilias* in his fallen state.

By defining his poem at its conclusion as an "anecdote," an entertaining through didactic allegory, "invented for its pith," Stevens recalls its main purpose: the disavowal of myth and the acceptance of reality. Allowing the reader to judge its veracity, Stevens slyly admits that if his "disguised pronunciamento" is accepted favorably (he may have felt the unpopularity of his theme, arriving so soon after "The Waste Land"), then his hero's failure to foil the "quotidian" acknowledges the only possible truth. If, however, the moral deduced from Crispin and his adventures appears too conciliatory, too slack for an age desiring mythic belief, then his example is "profitless" and his conclusions "distorting, proving what he proves / Is nothing." But the choice of rejecting Stevens' "anecdote" is severely limited, since he informs us of its inevitable conclusion: "What can all this matter since / The relation comes, benignly, to its end?" Since the commonplace is impervious to a tragic vision, there can be no lachrymose end.

"So may the relation of each man be clipped." Accordingly, the last epithet arrives in the form of a benediction and not as a cynical retort on human destiny as criticism has implied. "Clipped" with its raucous connotations of betrayal, does condemn harshly "all men" whose quest for a mythological paradise makes them pawns of their own illusions. The comic irony implicates Everyman who searches for transcendental reality instead of prudent wisdom. As a pun that neatly suggests comic reversals, "clipped" recalls all the setbacks that discouraged Crispin's metaphysical dreams. And finally the word relates to the process of entailment, which is lawyer's jargon for limiting rights to possess property. In the "Comedian" the "property" is reality, and what it resists are dominating mythologies and posturing heroics.

The vision of reality which the "Comedian" celebrates is shorn of the falsely ennobling effects of the "antique imagination." Yet, understandably, to diminish the efficacy of a myth which declares the belief in the Adamic perfection of man raises certain problems. It would appear that Stevens is in the position of deriding a false assumption, while morally required to posit some truth to take its place. Crispin's defeat before the "quotidian" facts of life is representative of this truth. Paradoxically, Crispin domesticated is Crispin recognized; his quest for truth is ironically successful, because it ends with self-knowledge which allows him to live realistically within his environment. In a wider context, Stevens offers to all the same journey through the failure of the past, which will eventually end in the discovery of a new world. The image that Stevens would substitute for Adam is therefore a youthful one:

It is the clear intelligence of the young man still bearing the burden of the obscurities of the intelligence of the old. It is the spirit out of its own self, not out of some surrounding myth, delineating with accurate speech the complications of which it is composed. For the Aeneas, it is the past that is Anchises. (*NA*)

From *The Centennial Review of Arts and Sciences,* 8 (1964), 465-77.

PETER L. McNAMARA

The Multi-Faceted Blackbird

WALLACE STEVENS' shrewd insight into sensuous reality is granted by most competent critics of modern poetry. Even if one was unaware of the poet's preoccupation with painting, his concern with color, texture, and shading would give evidence of painting's influence on his poetry. Emilie Buchwald emphasizes that "the whole of Stevens' work, to a greater degree than that of any other major poet of the first half of our century, attempts to replace representational seeing and relating, to come to terms with the possibilities and the dilemmas which the impressionist painters and symbolist poets encountered."[1]

Stevens' work reflects an alternate dilating and narrowing of poetic vision. At one extreme (as in "Thirteen Ways of Looking at a Blackbird") is the world of open-air landscapes; at the other, in a work such as "The Emperor of Ice Cream," that of the painter's studio. Whichever view of reality may concern him in any given poem, the vision grows out of the poet's acute awareness of the constant mutations in the external world. It is this awareness of change, of the myriad facets of existential reality, which Stevens intends to convey through his poetry. The need for man to be attentive to each element of reality is the message of a poem such as "Thirteen Ways of Looking at a Blackbird."

Critics have limited themselves principally, in considerations of this poem, to the symbolic significance of the blackbird. M. L. Rosenthal has suggested that it symbolizes "the inseparability of life and death in nature."[2] This seems valid; his refinements on this observation are not. The poem certainly suggests more than "a terrified sense of death's inexorability." That man is to die is important for Stevens; but he is more concerned with stressing the need, while the individual continues to live, of his appreciating reality. Awareness of death is important, but only as a stimulus to man's exploration of the things of this life. Much closer to the heart of the matter, it seems to me, is George McFadden's comment that "In 'Thirteen Ways of Looking at a Blackbird' Stevens showed how consciousness, through the imagination, can dominate brute, unmeaning being (black) by recomposing it as 'reality'—thirteen imagined, fully conscious views, each ideally possible in the mind of the viewer,

---

1. Emilie Buchwald, "Wallace Stevens: The Delicatest Eye of the Mind," *A. Q.* 14 (Summer 1962), 186.
2. M. L. Rosenthal, *The Modern Poets* (New York, 1960), 128.

each charged with feeling. As blackbirds are part of a landscape, he tells us, so death is a part of life."[3]

The opening lines of the poem employ contrast to point up the vibrant life possessed by the bird, suggestive of the concept that death and life are one and that the potentiality of death exists in all living things. We are made immediately aware, however, of Stevens' central concern; the poet pictures the blackness of the bird against the background of "twenty snowy mountains." The small, active eye of the bird, the "only moving thing," is played against the static majesty of inanimate nature. Already we have the key to the poem. Disturbed by man's self-satisfied neglect of nature, convinced that pleasure in it is the ultimate reward in a life that terminates in death, the poet emphasizes the importance of delving into life and seeing, understanding, and enjoying it fully. Contrasted here with the majestic mountains, the blackbird seems insignificant; knowledge of even the least significant aspect of nature is, however, the ideal to be realized.

Considering the blackbird in light of its representative symbolism, the poet is "of three minds." He concretizes these impressions in the image of "a tree / In which there are three blackbirds." Stevens' first thought is of the bird as it "whirled in the autumn winds." Here it is "a small part of the pantomime" of inanimate nature which merely reflects, in dumb show, the order which becomes meaningful when intellectually appreciated and verbally communicated. His second meditation relates the blackbird more explicitly to its place in the realm of animate creatures. If it is valid to say that "A man and a woman / Are one," that together they form the natural unit of humanity, then it is true in a more comprehensive sense that all existent things ("A man and a woman and a blackbird") are one in the order of nature. This fact makes it additionally important for man to become aware of the creatures and things around him, for in knowing things related to him, he is able to know himself more fully.

Stevens next attempts to discern whether the blackbird's message to man, symbolized by its song, is valid and valuable only on a surface level, or whether the observer will find its ultimate significance in contemplation. Certainly the appreciation of the surface "beauty of inflections" is important. Without at least such observation, man does not fulfill the purpose of life. But shouldn't man also try to capture "the beauty of innuendoes," the implications of which may be derived from an analysis of external nature? Because he is convinced that there is no deeper significance to life than the appreciation of natural beauty, the poet does "not know which" of the two beauties "to prefer."

Stevens next contemplates the unsatisfactory vision achieved by observing "the shadow of the blackbird" through the "barbaric glass" which obscures the average man's perceptions. The image calls to mind St. Paul's comment (I Corinthians 13:12) that in this life "we see through a glass, darkly." Stevens' man, like St. Paul, sees the shadow of reality, but loses sight of the object which

3. George McFadden, "Probings for an Integration: Color Symbolism in Wallace Stevens," *MP*, 58 (1961), 187.

produces it. Having chosen the study of nature as the ultimate source of truth, Stevens, much in the manner of an Old Testament prophet, asks the "thin men of Haddam," those men who seek in "golden birds" a higher glory, why they ignore the discernible reality of "the blackbird [that] / Walks around the feet / Of the women about you." It is interesting, in connection with the poet's reference to the "thin men of Haddam," that the town of Haddam, Connecticut was settled by the early Puritans. It is consistent with the poet's view of reality that he designates such men as "thin," in the sense that their vision of reality was distorted, their concerns being directed away from earthly reality.

Lest he be mistaken for a prosaic person, Stevens states that he knows "noble accents / And lucid, inescapable rhythms." He appreciates, in short, the appeal to the imagination which is made by the creative artist. Yet he is equally cognizant of the all-important fact "That the blackbird is involved / In what I know." If the poetic imagination is important, how much more important the intelligence which illumines for man the beauties of nature!

Despite all the efforts which man may make to know physical life, human limitation will, of course, frustrate his full understanding of it. Symbolically, "When the blackbird flew out of sight, / It marked the edge / Of one of many circles." The circle, a traditional symbol of wholeness, represents the limits of the observer's view, the outermost boundary of perception of life. The poet knows that such limitation is in him, that the realities of spatial immensity can never be fully known; this should not, however, discourage the effort to know.

Stevens sums up his message by commenting that if each of us was able to experience "the sight of blackbirds / Flying in a green light," he could be satisfied; even those of us who are "bawds of euphony," who seek truth in soporific visions, dreams or hopes of eternal life, would be jolted out of our misconceptions. Illumined reality, we note, appears "in a green light," suggestive to Stevens here as elsewhere of the vital force in nature which brings about harmony.

Instead of seeking understanding of this life, the average man will ride "over Connecticut / In a glass coach." Confident that technology has improved on nature in every way, he isolates himself from nature save when "a fear [pierces] him," when his sham view of the world is momentarily shaken by a contrasting vision of blackbirds. Though he only momentarily mistakes "his equipage / For blackbirds," soon becoming smug and self-satisfied once again, "The river is moving." Time (symbolized here by motion, in the philosophical sense of constant flux or change of state in existential reality) is passing, and with it the life of the unheeding man. Searching for happiness, he has overlooked its source, an imaginative harmony with and understanding of the world.

Will man rectify this limitation in his vision of earthly reality? Stevens seems to doubt this. His final contemplation is one in which "it was evening all afternoon. / It was snowing / And it was going to snow." Man continues to ignore nature, or sees it imperfectly, as if it were viewed at dusk, or in a storm, when his vision is obscured by falling snow. "The blackbirds sat / In the cedar-limbs," but the populace was and is too busy and uninterested to notice them. That people are happy in their delusions disturbs Stevens. He makes the effort in many of his poems to shake his unfeeling fellow humans from their lethargy. His lack of confidence in the success of his efforts is reflected in the dignified but overwhelming sense of futility of the closing lines of "Thirteen Ways of Looking at a Blackbird," certainly a key composition for revealing the poetic vision of Wallace Stevens.

From *College English*, 25 (1964), 446-48.

HAROLD C. ACKERMAN, JR.

Notes Toward An Explication of "Sea Surface Full of Clouds"

WHILE "Sea Surface" lacks the grandeur of length that one ordinarily associates with a major poem, it is one of Wallace Stevens' master works. "Sea Surface" is particularly repellent of analysis, though, because in it Stevens deliberately chooses to deal with the nuances of his subject, with relationships rather than with states or objects. He concerns himself, here, with the metaphorical processes of life rather than with life itself.

The concern is not unique with "Sea Surface": Stevens explores the function of metaphor in many poems and in some of his best-known pieces. Inevitably in these works, the concept of metaphor involves perception, and often multiple perceptions, as in "Thirteen Ways of Looking at a Blackbird." "Six Significant Landscapes," and "Variations on a Summer Day." These titles suggest imagism or impressionism. Yet in his own comment on the last of the three poems, we find Stevens asserting that "In a world permanently enigmatical, to hear and see agreeable things involves something more than mere imagism." His method seems to issue rather deliberately from his theory that an "absolute object slightly turned is a metaphor of the object," which itself echoes Valery's statement that "A metaphor is *what happens* when one *looks in a certain way*."[1] A poem providing twelve metaphors for a pineapple, then, is an experiment in perception and aesthetics, the chief goal of which is to determine what the mind can achieve. "Sea Surface" is a particularly luxurious and carefully-crafted experience, but in it Stevens tests the same theory.

We may understand how he goes about this by considering the whole structure of the poem. In "Sea Surface" whole structure is crucial because only within a rather predictable superstructure can the poet work emotions to such delicate shades. Stevens' framework for his little drama is the seascape which appears in so many of his poems: sea, sky, and man—man the observer, the listener, the perceiver. Moreover, this setting is developed in five sections nearly identical in structure, being composed of a few rhetorical constructions and even the same key nouns and verbs. Only the sensations, the adjectives, change throughout, though it is the genius of the poem that these in turn cause amazing changes in the repeated forms, the "surface" upon which the poet is intent. Thus, a key to the poem lies in the title itself: a seascape to be painted

---

1. As quoted in Frank Lentricchia, *The Gaiety of Language* (Berkeley, 1968), p. 38. I am indebted to the author for the connection of these statements.

five ways, and part of the meaning of the poem, as deduced from structure alone, is the profound effect of nuance and particulars upon the whole, and, in turn, upon the watcher of the whole.

To make this clearer, we might summarize the contents of each section.[2] There is an introductory passage of physical setting, the "given" so to speak, occupying the first seven lines; a seeing-hearing-beholding-evolving passage in which a human act in the least functionary sense of the word takes place, lines eight through eleven; a single, direct statement in French, line twelve; and a final description of motion in terms of deluge or transformation, the final six lines. Within this arrangement, each section develops one version of the mind of the beholder as it is expressed in French in each part. Finally, there is a gradually-realized difference in mood from section to section, a difference deriving at once from the perception of the beholder and from that which causes him to perceive as he does. This double source is created by Stevens' insistence upon the mutual importance of man and his encompassing universe. As he stated it in "The Comedian as the Letter C," "his soil is man's intelligence." We may say, then, that "Sea Surface Full of Clouds" describes the shades of atmosphere in a particular seaside world, but it depicts as well the phases of the mind as it continually changes and evolves with the world of which it is integral. And of course the mind changes that world by the nuances of meaning it discerns; Tehuantepec would not have meaning without it.

The mood of each of the five sections, therefore, may be explained by the mind of the speaker therein. In the first, he tells us that, "It was my child, my jewel, my soul." This admission, linked to the "rosy chocolate," the "suavity" of the ordinarily chaotic ocean, and the clouds that appear as "flotillas," offers the notion of a gem-like calm in which the poet and his objects are mutually immersed. It is the world of summer, the relationship that for Stevens suggested man at peace with himself and with nature.[3] But—as with the woman of "Sunday Morning"—the speaker is strangely unsatisfied, being too aware of his desires and of the natural perplexity of the ocean.

The second key line, "It was my brother of heaven, my life, my gold," is less reconcilable with the "jelly yellow" situation Stevens paints in part II. He definitely creates an air of deceptiveness: the yellow only "streaks" the deck, and all is "sham," "sheen," or "macabre." A certain gold terror pervades, something like an oriental dance-mask. Considering these details, one can read "brother of heaven" only in an ironic sense; if the beholder feels a brotherhood with this scene, he can only be thinking of the mutual distance of himself and his world from the traditional figure of a benevolent God. Religious themes are raised at least this early in the poem by details of sinister subtlety, the subtle treachery of the mind.

But the November of the third part is still another approach. Here Stevens offers the world of the Romantic as he understood the Romantic: gushing,

<hr />

2. Ronald Sukenick does this, without detailed explication, in *Wallace Stevens: Musing the Obscure* (New York, 1967), p. 228.
3. As in "The House Was Quiet and the World Was Calm," *CP*, 358-359.

ecstatic, unprincipled. Here the elements are music, flowers, and silver, which seduce the mind into "extase" and "amour." Almost unchecked, the lingering music and rainy hyacinth emit sensations as undefinable as those sunken clouds which assume shape after obscure shape. But at last the sea's relentless surging brings back a "sapphire" hue, brings back a beauty no less delightful for being more precise.

Of all the parts of the poem, II and IV most resemble each other, possibly in their "suggested malice." But again the line in French enables us to grasp their essential differences. "It was my faith, the unconcern divine," or, a translation perhaps closer to Stevens' acid wit, "the divine cool," The fourth section reads clearly in contrast with section I. Both suggest days of calm, but they differ as between "limpid" (I) and "musky" or "mallow" (IV); the former suggests a paradisal innocence, the latter a foreboding quietude. One thinks again of "Sunday Morning," of the "holy hush" imbued with an ironic weightiness from the arguments Stevens goes on to propound in that poem. Here, too, the day nearly cracks under the strain ("Would---"), except that Stevens will not proceed to meditate the agnostical possibilities of such a mallow morning. Once he has conjured the emotional situation, he allows it to be inundated by the rolling of sky and sea.

So far, Stevens has tried the suave, the ironic, the Romantic, the agnostic. But part IV raises the question, for those who had not already pondered it, as to which nuance, even in the most relative system of values, has the most meaning for the poet. And with the tone of satisfaction in part V, we are given something of an answer. "It was my bastard spirit, the prodigal." The frame of mind of the "Good clown" (elsewhere "fat Jocundus") seems to have held for Stevens the greatest personal delight, consisting of a less straining variant of the creative spirit with which the singer at Key West gives meaning to her experience. As an old man, one may still rage for order, certainly, but it is so much more convenient for the paunchy and slightly balding poet to be the juggler than the aesthete. This last section refers, then, to the droll. In exercising such a humor, Stevens has been labeled a dandy,[4] but he merely expresses his sense of the comic insofar as he possessed such a sense, and creates more than in any other section of the poem a moment of triumph. Of course, the triumph cannot last, no more than can a morning at sea off Tehuantepec.

After such an analysis, the question comes to mind whether or not Stevens may simply be practicing his scales. The question can arise as it cannot over, say, Eliot or Williams because of Stevens' unique poetical methods. That "Sea Surface" is a forceful poem and not merely an exercise, however, one may contend from the question inherent in the poem, in each section, of the Maker. If "Sea Surface" sets forth not only five seascapes but in fact five worlds, five of the mind's imagined places, it also deals with how those possibilities are created. The French phrase in each section always answers a question: "Who . . . evolved the sea blooms . . . ?" "Who . . . beheld the rising of the

4. Daniel Fuchs studies Stevens' dandyism and comments upon it in *The Comic Spirit of Wallace Stevens* (Durham, 1963). See especially pp. 11-14.

clouds / That strode submerged . . . ?" and finally, "What pistache one, ingenious and droll . . . ?" These questions contained for Stevens profoundest religious significance, as the total body of his work attests; for us they contain at least artistic importance.

Stevens chooses to answer in as metaphorical a manner as he can, but we may say with assurance that in the ordinary sense of the term no Divine personage is responsible. Instead, some human effort—an emotional experience, a memory, the imagination—dominates each part of the poem, fusing the disparate elements of a given November morning into a world swimming and charged with its own life. Each section, each nuance, has then its own movement, of which the imaginative perception forms the climax. But Stevens insists in this poem as he does not in various others upon the reality correspondent to the imagination. If man creates an order in this Tehuantepec November, he creates neither Tehuantepec nor November, and certainly not the sea. The possibilities of the mind have the one limitation of the possible transfigurations of blue in the sea, which for Stevens seems to have been a most handsome limitation.

Finally, it is the greatness of "Sea Surface Full of Clouds" that it conjures up five philosophies yet so insists upon the instruments to those visions that no one possibility can absolutely suffice. The poem is a whole unit not only because each part is a careful shading off from another, but because the series of related realms all dramatize the poem's ultimate message, as stated elsewhere, that

It can never be satisfied, the mind, never.

From *Concerning Poetry*, 2, No. 1 (Spring 1969), 73-77.

J. DENNIS HUSTON

"Credences of Summer": An Analysis

WALLACE STEVENS is never more clearly the poetic heir of Wordsworth than in "Credences of Summer," for this poem is essentially a rewriting of the Wordsworthian myth of reciprocity between man and nature. In it, too, is the nakedness characteristic of Wordsworth's most important works, where there is no mediating figure between the poet and the visibly concrete natural world; instead, the universe containing and contained in the consciousness of the observer is perceived directly, sometimes even without modification by image-ry. The cause of this particular effect is Stevens's desire to see the world in its essential "poverty" (p. 402),[1] to strike through the "fustian" (p. 375) outer garment of traditional thought to the "nakedness" (p. 402) beneath. By thus seeing "things as they are" (p. 165), the poet is able to discover, not to impose, the truth that comes as revelation in this poem. And although this truth is ·natural and not Biblical, it is nonetheless apocalyptic because it sets man "Free" (p. 378); simultaneously loosing the constricting bonds of solipsism and remov-ing the weight of human limitation, this truth proclaims the interdependence of the mind and nature. Green earth and blue imagination become one, and in this marriage there is for Stevens, as for Wordsworth, the possibility of a new creation, uniting heaven and earth in a "Now" that transcends the ordinary limits of time and place.

In his early poems Stevens is often concerned with showing how the human mind is suited to the world around it: the perceiving consciousness is one of his first published lyrics is that of a "snow man." In "Credences," however, he begins with this assumption and then examines the correlative idea, at last affirming its possibility in the triumphant eighth and ninth sections. Then, in the last part of the work, he makes actual what must be possible: the limiting characteristics of reality, space, and time, are transcended by their union and metamorphosis into form as fat "roseate characters, / . . . Complete in a completed scene, speaking / Their parts as in a youthful happiness" (p. 378). The elements of the external world, thus transformed into human figures by the poet's imagination, attest to the fact that nature is fitted to the human mind; and it is toward the miracle of this transformation that the whole poem moves.

From the beginning of "Credences" the problem of transience is implicit in the poet's proclamations of perfection: what is perfect in the natural world can

---

1. All page references are to *CP*.

remain so only momentarily. "The honey of heaven may or may not come, / But that of earth both comes and goes at once" (p. 15), Stevens writes in "Le Monocle de Mon Oncle," and the idea is also of central importance in "Credences." Even in his choice of title, for instance, Stevens suggests that beauty both comes and goes simultaneously. A "credence" is a belief, but it is also associated with a distinct kind of distrust. The word originally described a side table used for tasting the food of royal persons, to make certain it was free from poison, and occasionally "credence" referred to the actual process of tasting. Thus the title "Credences of Summer" implies both a belief and a distrust in the season: in the very ripeness of its beauty is hidden the poison of succeeding decay.

This idea, vaguely suggested by the ambiguous nature of the title, is much more apparent in the opening section. With the first word Stevens establishes his poem within time. "Now," he begins, and as he continues, he reminds the reader that summer is but one season in a cycle that has a very definite past and future:

> Now in midsummer come and all fools slaughtered
> And spring's infuriations over and a long way
> To the first autumnal inhalations. . . .

Other characteristics of the rhetoric of this first stanza also suggest the tension of opposing forces. In every verse there is at least one word with foreboding connotations: "slaughtered," "infuriations," "autumnal," "heavy with weight," "trouble." Even the time that Stevens is describing has contradictory implications associated with it because the festivals of midsummer are traditionally of two very different types, one celebrating the birth of love by pairing sweethearts and the other acknowledging the death of the spirit of vegetation. Stevens is, of course, not the first poet to make use of the ambiguous nature of midsummer. The combination of confusion and beauty in *A Midsummer Night's Dream* is obvious, and before Shakespeare Spenser contrasted Hobbinoll's joyful sense of paradise regained with Colin Clout's lovesickness in the June eclogue of *The Shepheardes Calender.*

In Stevens's setting, too, the imminent decay attending the perfection of natural fruition is suggested—by the juxtaposition of green and red colors. In the first stanza grass and roses are linked, and in the third grass that has become dry is mentioned soon after a reference to the "heart's core." These two colors, which are eventually united in the "sashed and seamed" costumes of the personae of summer, are of great symbolic importance to Stevens, green being for him the color of the summer vision; red, of the autumn one. And although these colors, like all of the symbols in Stevens's poetry, often defy interpretation, generally summer's green suggests imaginative fulfillment, while autumn's red implies the disjunction of imaginative desire and reality. In "Credences of Summer" the red colors of the autumnal vision, implicit from the beginning but not obviously defined until the ninth section, are encountered just as similar forces of natural change are met in Stevens's earlier work,

"Sunday Morning": they are viewed first with irony and later with a faith in the poetic power that results from the union of the natural world with the human imagination and heart.

The sense of joy that the natural world can transmit to the human mind is the principal subject of the first section, although the suggestion of the transience of natural perfection is developed as a subtle counterpoint to this idea. Facing the luxuriance of summer, Stevens says, man experiences a moment of satisfaction that is one of nature's gratuitous gifts to him. As he looks at the rich verdure, he can briefly forget that there is such a destructive force as time; he does not even have to remember other moments of happiness because the satisfaction of this moment, in nature's beauty and in the meaningfulness of human relationships, is absolute. Momentarily "the mind lays by its trouble . . . / and there is nothing left of time."

So satisfying, in fact, is this moment of joy that the viewer has an immediate sense of oneness with the natural world, a sense which cannot be described satisfactorily by the usual poetic devices of images and similes. Instead, the poet looks about with candor, content with the white nakedness of things as they are: "Trace the gold sun about the whitened sky / Without evasion by a single metaphor." Viewing the world in this way, Stevens sees with "the hottest fire of sight," and his vision is momentarily apocalyptic. In the fire that purifies by burning "everything not part of it to ash," he looks upon the realm that Yeats calls the Fifteenth Phase and that Blake calls Eden, where artist and art are indistinguishable. For Stevens, however, this moment of vision is not here achieved, as it is for Yeats and Blake, by the power of art. It is instead, like the bounding joy of the child when he first played among the hills near Tintern Abbey, a delight that results from a gratuitous gift of nature.

Such a gift, though, is not at all suited to analysis because to examine the particular aspects of experience contributing to this joy would be to remove oneself from it, and consequently to destroy it. In cautioning himself to "Postpone the anatomy of summer . . . ," Stevens is reaffirming Wordsworth's claim that "We murder to dissect." The joy that results from man's direct experience of natural beauty should preclude any concern with analysis; all that he needs to know is that no greater satisfaction can be offered him: "this is the centre that I seek." But since the satisfaction attending natural perfection must inevitably pass away, man tries to preserve it. Like Keats in the "Ode to Psyche," Stevens attempts to fix the luxuriance of the natural world "in an eternal foliage"—in a work of art that grows out of the union of the poet's imagination with nature. Art, however, is not nature, and because the foliage of art must necessarily be fixed, it escapes natural limitations only at the sacrifice of natural beauty; the art product is, paradoxically, barren in its eternally fertile state. In order to create a foliage filled with joy that is permanent, the artist has to create "the barrenness / Of the fertile thing that can attain no more." The last line of the second section should not, however, be interpreted as metaphor only, for the principal subject of this part of the poem is a moment of perfect satisfaction within the natural world; the speaker literally is experiencing the barrenness of a natural luxuriance that, having achieved perfection, can only produce succeeding decay.

This same experience is described in more metaphorical terms in the succeeding section. Here the summer scene is described principally in terms of space, the aspect of reality that has been subordinated to time in the first two parts. From the tower atop the "final mountain" the immenseness of space ("all the world") is brought within the range of the poet's vision. The mountain, as both Northrop Frye and Mircea Eliade have argued in different contexts, is characteristically a place of epiphany, for its position is between the mutable world of earth and the eternal world of the heavens. And here the mountain has just such symbolic significance. As an *axis mundi*,[2] a connection between heaven and earth located at the center of the world, it translates into space the psychological center mentioned in the second section.

At the top of Stevens's mountain there is a "natural tower," which is a manifestation of summer's perfection. Because it is made up of aspects of complete natural fulfillment—"green's green apogee"—this tower is "more precious than the view beyond." And, as the "Axis of everything," it incorporates time as well as space into itself. It is the "Now" of midsummer mentioned in the opening line of the poem, to which all past time in the year has moved in growth and from which all succeeding time will fall away in decay. That is why "the sun / Sleepless, inhales his proper air, and rests." Achieving the point in its ellipse when it is farthest north from the equator and shining most directly on the Northern Hemisphere, the sun must "rest" at the apex for a moment before it begins its return journey: "This is the refuge that the end creates." Like its obvious prototype, the bower atop Spenser's Garden of Adonis, this natural tower is the result not of art but of perfection in the natural process. Consequently, the old man here "reads no book." His sense of oneness with the external world is achieved not through the mediation of art but by direct and concrete experience: because "His ruddy ancientness / Absorbs the ruddy summer . . . ," he is himself a part of the natural perfection. The closing lines of this section humanize the luxuriant fulfillment described at the close of the preceding part:

> By an understanding that fulfils his age,
> By a feeling capable of nothing more.

The first three sections of "Credences of Summer," then, are variations on a theme—the joy that results from the direct experience of natural perfection. Beginning very specifically within time and implicitly suggesting the limitations attendant upon it, Stevens gradually moves his observer into a world of apparent timelessness, where space and time seem to assume eternal form. This movement is achieved principally by the indirect suggestion that the natural world is itself an artist: it blazons forth a perfection that satisfies even the desires of the imagination, bringing it to "the centre that I seek."

2. Mircea Eliade, *The Sacred and the Profane* (New York, 1959), pp. 36-39.

At the beginning of part 4 Stevens abruptly moves the reader back into a bounded realm: "One of the limits of reality. . . . " The fourth section of the poem is closely related to the first: both begin within a finite world, and, while describing its beauty, both affirm the possibility of transcending finite limitation. In its moments of perfection, the earth is enough; it is "all of paradise that we shall know" (p. 68). Looking at the hay fields in Oley, the poet, like Keats in the second stanza of "To Autumn," can know a moment of complete satisfaction with and within the natural world; and then there is no need for the creative power of the imagination. The "secondary senses of the ear," analogous to Coleridge's secondary imagination, are filled with the "Pure rhetoric of a language without words": no words are needed to correct the limitations of the natural world because momentarily it has none:

> The direction stops and we accept what is
> As good. The utmost must be good and is
> And is our fortune and honey hived in the trees
> And mingling of colors at a festival.

The fifth section of the poem is thematically tied to the second. In both Stevens's subject is the self-sufficiency of the moment that can be properly experienced only without the interference of any mediating figure between man and nature; even the usual poetic devices that depend, as Wordsworth emphasized, upon the power of memory have to be forsaken. "Stripped of remembrance," the day itself "displays its strength" and consequently should be viewed "Without evasion by a single metaphor." So perfect is the beauty that nature itself seems a work of art; for once the natural world accomplishes the task usually left to the poet, who "is *un amoureux perpetuel* of the world he comtemplates and thereby enriches." On this occasion, the day itself, and not the poet, "Enriches the year." It produces out of the marriage of the green and feminine earth with the ruddy and masculine sun a creation that is both a child and a work of art; it is the embodiment of all that the blue of the imagination would create:

> The more than casual blue
> Contains the year and other years and hymns
> And people, without souvenir.

"It is no doubt true," Stevens later writes in "Two or Three Ideas," "that the creative faculties operate alike on poems, gods and men up to a point. They are always the same faculties. One might even say that the things created are always the same things." A similar idea is being expressed poetically in the second and fifth sections of "Credences." The creation of nature, of earth and sun, is "one / Of the land's children"; but it is also, like a work of art, "the barrenness / Of the fertile thing that can attain no more." In its perfection all the limitations of the other days of the year are both transcended and implied—transcended because perfection momentarily excludes the fact of imperfection: the day "displays its strength— / The youth, the vital son, the

heroic power"; implied because that day "Contains the year": the natural cycle
of growth works to produce it, and the cycle of decay results from it.

This theme is expressed by the subtle and complex process of myth-making
that Stevens uses in the section. Like the myth which Northrop Frye suggests
that the poet uses in the seventh part of "Esthétique du mal," this one is formed
out of the implications of repetition. "One day enriches a year," Stevens begins,
and the reader cannot be certain what he means—a day could enrich a year
simply by adding to its length. But the day that is here the poet's concern has
a much more important function, which becomes clear only as Stevens develops
his myth: "One woman makes / The rest look down." Such a woman must
be a queen, before whom her subjects bow; and, by the implication of parallel
sentence structure, the poet suggests that the "One day" is somehow related
to the queen. In his next sentence he implies that it may also resemble a
mythical hero: "One man becomes a race, / Lofty like him, like him perpetual."
A major man may, like Adam or Aeneas, found a race that embodies his own
characteristics. But to speak of major man in Stevens's poetry is always to imply
a reference to the natural force from which major man derives his origin, the
sun. More certainly than any traditional hero, the sun becomes a race whose
characteristics are derived from it: "we are men of the sun" (p. 137), and "All
things in the sun are sun" (p. 104). Thus, the one day that enriches a year is
by implication related to a queen, to a mythical hero, and to the sun. How
Stevens is using these implied relationships becomes apparent as the poem
continues.

"Or do the other days enrich the one?" Stevens is here facing the old
philosophical problem of the relationship between the many and the one, and
his succeeding verses show that he thinks the relationship is built upon an
interdependence. The one fosters the many, just as the many produce the one:
the day is born out of the year, but it "Contains the year and other years." To
demonstrate the truth of this idea, Stevens uses the example supplied by a
colony of bees:

> And is the queen humble as she seems to be,
> The charitable majesty of her whole kin?

Is the queen bee, the poet asks, the mother of her whole kin because of her
gratuitousness? The question forces the reader himself to provide the answer,
which is: No. The queen produces all the other bees, but she is dependent upon
them for her survival, as they are dependent upon her for their existence.
Because the queen cannot get her own food, she needs the workers that she
produces. Now, having established the nature of the relationship between the
one and the many, Stevens is ready to complete his myth. From the marriage
of lofty father sun with queen mother earth comes the birth of midsummer
day—"The bristling soldier, weather-foxed, who looms / In the sunshine is
a filial form and one / Of the land's children"—that enriches the year, because
it contains in its perfection both the fulfilled potentialities of growth and the

necessities of decay that define the other days in the year, the other unions of earth and sun.

When nature produces such art, there is no need for man to attempt imaginative creation; he needs only to look about him. Like the third section of "Credences," the sixth is a description of natural perfection, expressed in metaphorical language. The various manifestations of summer are not, however, viewed as a "natural tower" as they were in the earlier section; instead, they are seen as a "rock," a symbol that has a number of implications important in this context. First, in Christian mythology, the rock is associated with the revealed truth of Christ promised by the Church; and, though Stevens overtly rejects the doctrines of all organized religions, he can appropriate a religious symbol for his own particular poetic purposes. "It is the truth," he says. Second, the rock has associations with truth in Greek as well as in Christian mythology. The sacred stone, or *omphalos,* of the Greeks was supposed to mark the center of the earth, and there the Delphic oracle, the seat of prophetic wisdom, was located. Third, and perhaps most important, the rock, like the beautiful midsummer day, can be considered a natural product of the marriage of earth and sun, for rock is formed out of sediment that has been subjected to the intense heat of fire, whose source is the sun. The "rock of summer" is, then, the full perfection of the union of earth and sky; momentarily, the eternal and the mutable worlds are united, and there is no need for art or for the promises of religion, the "hermit's truth." The earth itself is enough:

> It is the visible rock, the audible,
> The brilliant mercy of a sure repose,
> On this present ground, the vividest repose,
> Things certain sustaining us in certainty.

But although natural fulfillment gives the viewer a momentary illusion of timelessness, the perfection passes: the sudden appearance of irony at the close of the sixth section signals the onset of the poet's struggle with the problems of the autumnal vision. This irony is produced by an abrupt change in Stevens's technique. Consistently in the first six sections of the poem, he has refrained from using similes to achieve an effect of concreteness; nothing seems to stand between the poet and the natural world. As Northrop Frye has demonstrated, the power of Stevens's poetry most often results from direct statement or from the evocative use of metaphor; he carefully avoids similes because they detract from the immediacy of experience, from the "sharp flash, / The vital, arrogant, fatal, dominant X" (p. 288). Above all, Stevens's concern in writing poetry that is a "theory of life" (p. 486) is to avoid "the intricate evasions of as" (p. 486). There is, however, something intricately evading about the last line of part 6 in "Credences." In it the poet replaces metaphor and direct statement with simile:

> It is the rock of summer, the extreme,
> A mountain luminous half way in bloom

> And then half way in the extremest light
> Of sapphires flashing from the central sky,
> As if twelve princes sat before a king.

The closing verse is hollow sounding. If its quick singsong meter does not consciously echo the Mother Goose rhyme about four-and-twenty blackbirds, it at least provides a distinct contrast to the stately, Miltonic verse which precedes it. With the irony of this line, Stevens prepares his reader for the beginnings of the autumnal vision that is to follow in the next section. And as the poet examines the question of how man is to meet the passing of beauty within the external world, poetry, and not nature, becomes for the first time in this work the subject of the poem.

Trying to fix permanently in art an experience of complete natural satisfaction, a group of singers carol "unreal songs." Significantly, too, they sing while they are "in the woods," where they have gone to get away from the summer fields that are celebrated in their song. Poetry about natural fulfillment must always be born out of the memory of that fulfillment, not out of the immediate experience itself, for desire is a necessary complement to the poetic process, and there can be no desire in the face of perfection:

> They sang desiring an object that was near,
> In face of which desire no longer moved.

But there is another reason why these singers are "in the woods": they are there figuratively because they do not know the proper way to write poetry. "Secure," they sing "unreal songs." Like the term "Romantic," the word "unreal" has contradictory meanings for Stevens. Northrop Frye has remarked that the poet uses it to describe the shaping power that the imagination brings to reality in the process of transforming experience into art. The unreal in imaginative perception is, then, the power which makes a man a poet. But the word can also have pejorative connotations because, if the unreal is not used for perceiving the real but is instead turned in upon itself, it will create only spectacle. "The imagination," Stevens argues in one of his earliest essays, "loses vitality as it ceases to adhere to what is real. When it adheres to the unreal and intensifies what is unreal, while its first effect may be extraordinary, that effect is the maximum effect it will have" (NA, 6). In part 7 of "Credences," the songs of the singers deep in the woods are unreal because they are not firmly grounded in reality; instead "The singers had to avert themselves / Or else avert the object." Turning away from the real and ignoring the decay that must inevitably follow natural fulfillment, they sing of a perfection that needs no song. In the security of the woods they ignore the violence of reality and content themselves with the "unreal."

Opposed to the singers' philosophy that finds in art an escape from reality, is the voice that, halfway through this section, introduces a markedly different rhetoric and tone. Security is replaced by tension:

> Three times the concentred self takes hold, three times
> The thrice concentred self, having possessed
>
> The object, grips it in savage scrutiny,
> Once to make captive, once to subjugate
> Or yield to subjugation, once to proclaim
> The meaning of the capture . . .

The voice here is most certainly the poet's, and the subject may be nothing less than Stevens's own poetic creed. Artistic creation he argues, evolves out of the struggle between the individual mind and the external world that threatens to obliterate its identity. In a universe of mutability, the significance of the individual perceiving consciousness is threatened by the pressure of reality: " . . . in speaking of the pressure of reality, I am thinking of life in a state of violence" (*NA*, 26). Once the poet has recognized the threat that he faces from the external world, once he has "possessed / The object" and with "savage scrutiny" made it captive, he must bring his imagination into the battle against this external violence to discover whether or not the self has any singular significance. In the course of this struggle to subjugate or yield to subjugation, he must employ "a violence from within that protects us from a violence without. It is the imagination pressing back against the pressure of reality. It seems, in the last analysis, to have something to do with our self-preservation" (*NA*, 36). And, at the conclusion of the battle between the imagination and the external world, the poet must proclaim the result in his poem. Only in this way can he bring to mankind a truth whose purpose is "not to console / Nor sanctify, but plainly to propound" (p. 389). It is a truth whose result is to set man "Free" (p. 378) because it is apocalyptic: "Poetry is a revelation in words by means of words" (*NA*, 33).

Once man has found the means by which to discover revealed truth, the apocalypse follows quickly. "The trumpet of morning blows in the clouds and through / The sky": it is Stevens's own particular trumpet of revelation. Born out of the natural world, it proclaims the sanctity of earth that man must learn to substitute for his belief in the sanctity of heaven, which is merely the unreal creation of another age:

> The trumpet cries
> This is the successor of the invisible. . . .
>
> This, in sight and memory,
> Must take its place, as what is possible
> Replaces what is not.

Then, in order to demonstrate the inadequacy of a concept of heaven that grew out of the aesthetic projections of another age, Stevens ironically turns the characteristic poetic device of that era against its beliefs. Milton's stately alliterative technique is used to reduce the sound of thunder claps to that of breaking glass and fallen angels to mere "tumblers." Describing Christ's victory in the war in heaven, Milton proclaims:

> Full soon
> Among them he arriv'd; in his right hand
> Grasping ten thousand Thunders. . . .
> [*Paradise Lost* 6.834-36]

Stevens's description of an end to the meaning of Christian belief is an ironic echo of Milton's verses:

> The resounding cry
> Is like ten thousand tumblers tumbling down
> To share the day.

The real significance of the cock's trumpet cry for Stevens is simply that it is *heard* as one of the number of sounds—"As that of a personage in a multitude"—that signifies the dawn of a new day. In order for sounds to be sounds, Stevens thus implies, they must be *heard*, just as objects must be named before they actually become objects: "A poet's words are of things that do not exist without the words" (*NA,* 32). Once again, with faith in the importance of the "one," Stevens is returning to the question raised by the myth that he made in the fifth section of his poem: What is the relationship between the one and the many, between the individual perceiving mind and the external world of nature about it? The answer that the poet offers to this question is the same one earlier supplied by Wordsworth in "The Recluse":

> How exquisitely the individual Mind
> . . . to the external World
> Is fitted:—and how exquisitely, too— . . .
> The external World is fitted to the Mind.

Not only is the human being, as in the first section of "Credences," often dependent upon the natural world for his reality, but the world is dependent upon him as well: before it can exist, it must be perceived.

> The trumpet supposes that
> A mind exists, aware of division, aware
> Of its cry as clarion. . . .
> Man's mind grown venerable in the unreal.

The word "venerable" in the last line of this section is particularly suited to Stevens's purposes because of its associations both with old age and religion, for it is a religion grown old that the poet is here rejecting. Too long contented with the outworn myths of another age, modern man has avoided the "pressure of reality." Like the singers in the woods, he has averted himself from the

objective world in order to inhabit an unreal one. But, though man's tendency
to believe in the imaginative creations of another age has divorced him from
the world of present reality, he need not remain so separated. Those same
imaginative powers that have allowed him to grow "venerable in the unreal"
can be the source of his new vision of truth. When it is turned upon the
external world, his imaginative capacity, the "unreal" that he brings to experience, is proof of the interdependence of the self and nature. Only from man's
perception of it does the external world derive its reality: "The trumpet
supposes that / A mind exists, aware of division . . . / Man's mind." The same
idea is more fully expressed in Stevens's essays:

> . . . the imagination is the faculty by which we import the unreal into what
> is real. . . . It is not only that the imagination adheres to reality, but, also,
> that reality adheres to the imagination and that the interdependence is
> essential. (*NA,* 150, 33)

Often when Stevens is expressing an idea of immense importance to him,
his poetic tone verges on irony. That is what happens at the beginning of the
ninth section: "Fly low, cock bright, and stop on a bean pole." The rhetoric
of the verse begins as if it were going to soar with no middle flight, but the
sound and sense of the words abruptly bring the reader back to earth, which
is exactly where the poet wants him to be. Perched on the bean pole that, like
the mountain and the rock earlier, is another symbol of the *axis mundi,* the
cock beholds the beginnings of the autumnal vision. Soon the sun will begin
to redden his breast, and as he looks about, he recognizes the transience of the
natural condition: "The gardener's cat is dead, the gardener gone." He may
even, like Stevens, "detect / Another complex of other emotions" as the
summer complex falls apart and natural fulfillment passes. But the bird, who,
as singer and as trumpet of a prophecy, is to be identified with the poet, accepts
the necessity and beauty of this change because it is change that defines life,
the only paradise that man can know. And in this very recognition of change
is the proof of the interdependence of man and nature: there can be change
only so long as there is a mind "aware of division" to perceive it. This is what
is implied by the presence of the voice that makes a "sound, / Which is not
part of the listener's own sense" at the end of the ninth section. In one way,
that voice is the bird's, nature's, coming from outside man and not part of his
sense; it is what the external world gives to man. But in another way that voice
is the poet's, man's, saying something that is not part of listening nature's
sense; it is what man gives to the external world. Like the bird's cry that brings
"A new knowledge of reality" at the end of *The Collected Poems,* the sound is
both of man and nature. So closely are the one and the many related, in fact,
that nature is as human as man is natural. That is why the world of Wallace
Stevens' poetry is large enough to include both the snow man and the fat,
roseate characters of summer.

From *Modern Philology,* 67 (1970), 263-72.

MARJORIE PERLOFF

Irony in *The Rock*

DISCUSSION OF Wallace Steven's final volume of poems, *The Rock* (1954), has been unnecessarily solemn and doctrinaire. On the one hand, much has been made of the poet's debt to various philosophers. Marius Bewley, for example, writes, "Poetry is not metaphysics, but there is such a thing as a philosophical poet, and Stevens deserves this title."[1] For Bewley, Stevens is essentially an American Transcendentalist whose verse is "on the point of tipping into mysticism." The Platonic influence has been discussed by A. Alvarez, the Santayana influence by Norman Holmes Pearson; and Frank Doggett has noted, in a recent article, that there are also parallels between Stevens' thought and the doctrines of Bergson, Whitehead, and William James.[2] On the other hand, Stevens's late poetry is often deplored precisely because it does seem so "philosophical." Thus, Roy Harvey Pearce argues that Stevens finally abandons the real world completely for an "ultimate humanism" which paradoxically "leads him toward a curious dehumanization." Stevens's late poems are "the poems of a man who does nothing but make poems."[3] "The tragedy," Pearce says, "is that to say yes, Stevens had in the end to say no to so much—to jettison the creative for the decreative, the actual for the possible, men for man, the world for the Rock." Pearce's view is echoed by Howard Nemerov, who complains, "particulars are now being treated as though . . . they were already dissolved in generality," and by G. S. Fraser, who declares that the late poems lack "the urgency of human passion" and "the highest tension" and are consequently "like commentaries on themselves that could be added to forever, section by section, like expanding book-cases."[4]

All these approaches seem to miss a basic point about *The Rock,* namely that the mode of the last poems is essentially the ironic mode: the speaker in these poems is less a philosopher than a sophisticated, aloof spectator, whose attitude to the various "isms" he reflects upon is highly ambivalent. The poems in *The Rock* are marked by what might be called a "double vision" of material reality, the Stevensian "things as they are." For if the imagination is able, in brief

---

1. Bewley, "The Poetry of Wallace Stevens," *Commonweal,* LXII, 622 (Sept. 23, 1955).

2. A. Alvarez, *Stewards of Excellence* (New York, 1958), p. 130; Norman Holmes Pearson, "Wallace Stevens and 'Old Higgs,' " *Trinity Review,* VIII, 35-36 (Spring, 1954); Frank Doggett, "Wallace Stevens' River That Flows Nowhere," *Chicago Review,* XV, 67-80 (Autumn, 1962).

3. Pearce, *The Continuity of American Poetry* (Princeton, N.J., 1961), p. 413.

4. Howard Nemerov, "The Poetry of Wallace Stevens," *Sewanee Review,* LXV, 13 (Winter, 1957); G. S. Fraser, review of *The Rock, Partisan Review,* XXII, 270 (Spring, 1955).

moments, to transform reality into something radiant, the vision is only momentary and fragmentary, and it is always accompanied or succeeded by what Northrop Frye has called Stevens's "autumn vision." As Frye puts it, "To perceive 'reality' as dingy or unattractive is itself an imaginative act . . . but an ironic act, an irony deepened by the fact that other modes of perception are equally possible . . . and there can be no question of accepting only one as true."[5] Stevens himself, as Frye has observed, states the basic dilemma in a poem from *Ideas of Order* (1936):

> From oriole to crow, note the decline
> In music. Crow is realist. But, then,
> Oriole, also, may be realist. (*CP*, 150)

The ironic mode is not, of course, peculiar to Stevens's last works: in the opening poem of *Harmonium* (1931), "Earthy Anecdote" (*CP*, 3), the tone is generally light and playful, but the symbol of the order that transforms chaos in the course of the poem is the strange and menacing firecat. In "Sunday Morning" (*CP*, 66), despite the imagery of luxuriance and splendor, there is a great deal of ironic qualification: the "green freedom of a cockatoo" is actually fixed in the pattern of the rug, the much-worshiped sun turns out to be "an old chaos of the sun," and the pigeons make "ambiguous undulations as they sink / Downward to darkness on extended wings." Even in the early poetry, it seems, Stevens is never quite what Randell Jarrell calls him with reference to *The Rock:* "the poet of well-being," "all Windhover and no Jesuit."[6] In Stevens' second volume, *Ideas of Order* (1936), the tone of the poems in *The Rock* is prefigured in a remarkable piece, "How to Live. What To Do" (*CP*, 125), in which the wind, first a frightening and ominous sound, becomes paradoxically "a heroic sound / Joyous and jubilant and sure." By the time we come to *The Auroras of Autumn* (1950), we find a great many poems in the final mode—particularly "Puella Parvula," "What We See Is What We Think," "The Novel," and "St. John and the Back-Ache."

But there is also, especially in the middle period, a second strain of poetry which is more directly philosophical and doctrinal, and which perhaps deserves the strictures of Pearce and Nemerov. Typical of this strain is the famous anthology piece, "The Idea of Order at Key West" (*CP*, 128). This poem ostensibly deals with "The maker's rage to order words of the sea," but, as Denis Donohue points out, the poor sea (reality) never gets its due within the confines of the poem, which thus becomes "a painfully narrow definition . . . of the liaison between the agent and the environment."[7] We are *told* that

5. Frye, "The Realistic Oriole: A Study of Wallace Stevens," *Hudson Review*, X, 359 (Autumn, 1957).

6. Jarrell, "The Collected Poems of Wallace Stevens," *Yale Review*, XLIV, 344, 348 (March, 1955).

7. Donohue, "Wallace Stevens and the Abstract," *Studies* (Irish Quarterly Review), XLIX, 392 (Winter, 1960).

the song of the insubstantial heroine makes order out of the chaos of the observed reality (ocean, sky, wind, etc.). But why and in what sense does she become a "maker"? Stevens does not dramatize the "making" process; he simply insists that:

> She was the single artificer of the world
> In which she sang. And when she sang, the sea,
> Whatever self it had, became the self
> That was her song, for she was the maker.

The climactic phrase, "Oh blessed rage for order," is not intrinsic to this poem in which order has been achieved, not by means of "rage," but with great ease. Northrop Frye, one of the few critics who does not admire "Key West," points out that Stevens's "deliberately magical" poems like this one "have the special function of expressing a stasis or harmony between imagination and reality, and hence have something of a conscious rhetorical exercise about them." Frye's implication is that Stevens's central theoretical principle, namely that poetry is "an interdependence of the imagination and reality as equals" (*NA*, 27), must be dramatized, not merely stated. The poem itself should ideally be the "song" that makes "order" out of the flux of reality.

In *The Rock*, there are still a few "deliberately magical" poems, such as "The Song of Fixed Accord," "The Planet on the Table," and "The Poem That Took the Place of a Mountain," but the bulk of the poems exhibits precisely that "rage for order" which was absent from "Key West." It might be useful to begin our consideration of *The Rock* by looking at the widely discussed "The World as Meditation" (*CP*, 520), a poem at once very similar to and very different from "Key West."

"The World as Meditation" is generally read as a serious account of the imagination's creation of an invented world, more satisfying than the real one. Joseph N. Riddel's reading is typical:

> Penelope is like the poet whose search for fulfillment discovers only his own powers; she is, it appears, the self seeking reunion with the world from which it is separated, from Ulysses who is at once reality and its source. Ulysses is the sun which brings only its own presence, the vital energy of day or life, but that is assurance enough for the subjective self, which, however conscious of the abyss between itself and nature, manages composure in meditative union with its external paramour.[8]

Is the poem, then, simply a restatement of its epigraph, the violinist Enesco's

---

8. Riddel, "Wallace Stevens' 'Visibility of Thought,'" *PMLA*, LXXVII, 489-490 (Sept., 1962). Cf. Louis L. Martz, "Wallace Stevens: The World as Meditation," *Yale Review*, XLVII, 518 (June, 1958): " . . . her [Penelope's] imagination of Ulysses, her constant meditation of reunion with the man she constantly creates in her mind, this power presses back, composes within herself a world of value and order."

reference to the "rêve permanent, qui ne s'arrête ni nuit ni jour," the dream which distinguishes the mind of the artist from other minds? What, we must ask, is the speaker's attitude to Penelope's meditation?

Ulysses is first described as the "interminable adventurer," a rather ironic reference, for we usually think only of events, not of people, as being "interminable." In Penelope's dream world, the speaker remarks, the trees do not blossom; they are merely "mended" and winter is "washed away." Penelope is not a queenly figure; she is dressed in "cretonnes." Her imagined future with Ulysses is defined in intentionally trite language: "Two in a deep-founded sheltering, friend and dear friend," a phrase echoed later in "Yet they had met, / Friend and dear friend and a planet's encouragement." In the sixth tercet, Penelope begins to wonder whether the approaching "form of fire" is really Ulysses or whether it is "only the warmth of the sun on her pillow." The next two lines contain the core of the poem:

> The thought kept beating in her like her heart.
> The two kept beating together. It was only day.

The words "only day" are the key words here. Penelope's dream, unlike Enesco's "rêve permanent," is only a daydream, and the poem is an ironic version of the epigraph: the daydream serves as a comment on the dream. In this context, "The barbarous strength within her would never fail," a line which is usually read as an affirmation of Penelope's triumph, has an almost comic ring, for Penelope's strength is at best a very dubious quality. Unlike the woman in "The Idea of Order at Key West," who easily "makes" her song of the sea, Penelope does not arrive at her goal. The imagination, Stevens suggests, can do a great deal but not as much as people like Enesco think it can. The title of the poem is, then, finally ironic. "Meditation" does not constitute a "world"; Ulysses, the reality, "interminably" eludes it.

A second example of Stevens's deepening irony in *The Rock* may be found in comparing "One of the Inhabitants of the West" (*CP*, 503) to an earlier poem which deals with the same theme, "Martial Cadenza" (*CP*, 237). In "Martial Cadenza," the speaker sees the evening star, in its solitude and lonely splendor, as a symbol of the eternal renewal of life and hence of the imagination:

> Itself
>
> Is time, apart from any past, apart
> From any future, the ever-living and being,
> The ever-breathing and moving, the constant fire,
>
> .   .   .   .   .
>
> The vivid thing in the air that never changes,
> Though the air change.

In "One of the Inhabitants of the West," this theme is handled more

indirectly. A basic contrast is established between the "blaze" of the single,
isolated evening star (the inhabitant of the West), which is visible at the
"earliest fall of night," and the gaudy opulence of a cluster of stars ("horrid
figures of Medusa") in the constellation Perseus, which is still hidden from
sight. The evening star (the planet Venus) has, of course, only reflected light,
while the "real" stars have a "well-rosed two-light / Of their own." Yet, as
the "reader of the text" realizes, the planet whose light is merely reflected light
seems, in its very apartness from the darkness that falls over Europe and the
"sheeted Atlantic," paradoxically brighter than the constellation with its own
bright lights could ever be. Brightness is, then, not an absolute quality but a
matter of context, of relationship. It is the perceived relationship of light to
light, and of light to darkness, that defines the value of "this one star's blaze,"
and so there is no need for the slightly pretentious list of epithets for the star
which Stevens provides in "Martial Cadenza."

In "Martial Cadenza," the narrator's reaction to the star is very serene and
confident:

> . . . I walked and talked
> Again and lived and was again, and breathed again
> And moved again and flashed again, time flashed again.

But in "One Of The Inhabitants," the moment of insight seems fragmentary
and muted. "Our divinations" are, at best, fleeting; our reason quickly recalls
that "So much guilt lies buried / Beneath the innocence / Of autumn days."

"Prologues to What Is Possible" (*CP*, 515)[9] is a much more extended and
compelling treatment of our "mechanisms of angelic thought"; one might call
it Stevens's "Immortality Ode." Marius Bewley believes that "Prologues" is an
Emersonian poem, describing Stevens's "inner illumination in terms that are
either frankly or approximately mystical." In Part I, the metaphor of the
journey in the boat "built out of stones that had lost their weight," which is
"carried forward by waves resembling the bright backs of rowers / Gripping
their oars, as if they were sure of the way to their destination," is used to convey
a moment of insight into supernatural reality; the speaker perceives "a
meaning" which is "Removed from any shore, from any man or woman." The
self is momentarily transcended in an "approximately mystical" experience, as
Bewley says.

But Part II opens with the short, striking sentence, "The metaphor stirred
his fear." The speaker comes down to earth: " . . . he knew that likeness of
him extended / Only a little way, and not beyond. . . . " There is, ultimately,
no "meaning" that is "Removed from any shore, from any man or woman,"
for the only "intimations of immortality" come, paradoxically, from our own
daily, palpable experience, from "The way a look or a touch reveals its unex-

9. Note that the evening star motif, just discussed with reference to "One of the Inhabitants,"
appears in "Prologues" in lines 16-17.

pected magnitudes." We recall Stevens's dictum: "The imagination loses vitality as it ceases to adhere to what is real" (*NA, 6*).

It is important to note that, contrary to Bewley's statement, "Prologues" cannot be called a Transcendentalist poem. Emerson, like Stevens, takes the real, the material, as his starting point and discovers that nature is the symbol of spirit, but his emphasis is quite different from that of Stevens. While Stevens talks of "A flick which added to what was real," Emerson typically asserts, in a much more positive tone, "Standing on the bare ground—my head bathed by the blithe air and uplifted into infinite space—all mean egotism vanishes. I become a transparent eyeball; I am nothing; I see all; the currents of the Universal Being circulate through me; I am part and parcel of God."[10]

Emerson's words are full of resolution and conviction, a conviction nowhere to be found in "Prologues." Even the metrical form of Part II suggests Stevens's hesitation: the eight-stress line of Part I is still the norm, but the range is from six stresses per line (line 8) to ten per line (line 2). The regularity of Part I is thus replaced by irregularity in Part II. The title of the poem is, in this context, ironic: the "possible" is, as the poem has shown, also the "impossible." It is natural, Stevens suggests, for man to want to transcend the self, and in certain moments of illumination he feels he can do so, but such "spiritual" experience is, in the end, an illusion. One is reminded at this point of his discussion of Plato's myth of the charioteer in the *Phaedrus;* it is a beautiful myth, Stevens says, but because it "does not adhere to what is real" (*NA, 6*), it is ultimately "gorgeous nonsense" (*NA, 4*). The metaphor of the boat journey is as remote as Plato's myth, and the speaker of Part II knows that he must reject it.

Transcendentalism receives more direct treatment in the enigmatic poem, "Looking Across the Fields and Watching the Birds Fly" (*CP,* 517). Mildred E. Hartsock reads the last tercet as containing Stevens's credo that "The duty of men is to go 'as far as they can.' "[11] This reading is probably the result of the unfortunate habit of detaching lines or groups of lines from Stevens's poetry and treating them as so many more "Adagia." Surely the final tercet refers to the thoughts of Mr. Homburg, whose foolish name (humbug? hamburger? Homburg hat?) suggests that he is not likely to be a mask for the poet. Bewley has been the first to point out that Mr. Homburg of Concord is, no doubt, meant to be Emerson, and that the reference to the "pensive nature," the "mechanical / and slightly detestable *operandum*" of the third tercet is most probably a reference to the Emersonian Over-Soul. Bewley, however, implies that there is only one speaker in the poem, when there are, in fact, two: 1) Homburg (ll. 4-11), whose view is that there is a spiritual reality, "free / From man's ghost, larger and yet a little like . . . "; and 2) a "new scholar replacing an older one" (l. 37), whose thoughts are contained in lines 12-36, the three dots at the end of line 11 signalling the transition. The view of the "new

10. "Nature," *The Complete Essays of Emerson* (Modern Library College Ed., New York, 1950), 6.
11. Hartsock, "Wallace Stevens and the Rock," *Personalist,* XLII, 72 (Winter, 1961).

scholar" begins at the opposite pole from Homburg's; we must, he says, adhere to

> What we know in what we see, what we feel in what
> We hear, what we are, beyond mystic disputation. . . . (ll. 19-20)

But, curiously enough, the speaker's thoughts move further and further away from the present (see ll. 28-30), and finally they are not very different from Homburg's thoughts. At this point, the speaker becomes annoyed with himself and calls his own rumination a "fantasia" (l. 37). He dismisses it, and in the last two tercets we return to Mr. Homburg, who tries to confine the essence of nature in a neat little container ("The mannerism of nature caught in a glass"), until it becomes only "a spirit's mannerism." Since they are "caught in a glass," the "things going as far as they can" (l. 45) cannot, of course, go very far.

Neither Homburg's doctrine nor the speaker's "fantasia" seems to provide a ready solution. Can man, then, do no more than the title of the poem suggests, that is, quite literally look across the fields and watch the birds fly? There is no resolution of these alternatives in the poem, only an ironic juxtaposition. There are, one surmises, still at least "thirteen ways of looking at a blackbird."

I should like to consider next a group of "life cycle" poems in *The Rock;* these dramatize what Frank Doggett has called "the turning instant of the now,"[12] when, to use Northrop Frye's terminology, the winter vision gives way to the spring vision, the summer vision is replaced by the autumn vision, and so on.[13] According to Doggett, this is the moment "when the meaningless becomes awareness, when attention selects and interprets external chaos . . .," but, as we shall note, the shift works both ways: sometimes awareness becomes the meaningless.

The most interesting of these poems is the little-known "The Green Plant" (*CP,* 506). In the first three stanzas the narrator surveys, from the vantage point of his window, the decaying late-autumn foliage. The stasis of October ripeness[14] is dissolved:

> Silence is a shape that has passed.
> Otu-bre's lion-roses have turned to paper

12. Doggett, "Wallace Stevens' Later Poetry," *ELH,* XXV, 150 (June, 1958).

13. The most important of the "life cycle" poems in *The Rock* is, of course, the title poem, "The Rock." Since an adequate analysis of this long and complex poem would take a great deal of space, and since it has already received extensive discussion, I prefer in this essay to talk about some of the shorter poems which have, so far, received almost no attention. For comment on "The Rock," see Pearce, pp. 409-411; Frye, p. 362; Jarrell, p. 342; Hartsock, p. 74; Riddel, p. 491; Frank Kermode, *Wallace Stevens* (New York, 1961), p. 125; and Ralph Mills, "Wallace Stevens: The Image of the Rock," *Accent,* XVIII, 75-89 (Spring, 1958).

14. The personification of October as a showman-vendor, who must resort to hawking dead flowers, is particularly apt here.

> And the shadows of the trees
> Are like wrecked umbrellas.

The next two stanzas carry out the logical implications of the first, but, in
·Stanza 4, the narrator turns to the indoor scene:

> Except that a green plant glares, as you look
> At the legend of the maroon and olive forest,
> Glares, outside of the legend, with the barbarous green
> Of the harsh reality of which it is part.

The glaring plant is part of the "harsh reality," but, ironically, its green is
not the green of spring renewal; it is "barbarous green" because the indoor
plant, artificially cultivated, is really less, not more, alive than the dying autumn
foliage. As the plant's "reality" impinges upon the narrator's mind, a strange
transformation takes place: the ugly outdoor scene becomes a "legend" into
which the plant cannot enter; the "wrecked umbrellas" become a "forest," and
"red" and "yellow" become the more refined "maroon" and "olive." The
"effete vocabulary of summer" does say something after all.

Notice that in "The Green Plant" "things as they are" are not simply
transformed by a "blue guitar" (CP, 165); rather, one aspect of reality transforms
the other, and both are fused by an imaginative act which is the poem itself.
The creation of order is not only described; it is dramatized. There is also the
implication in "The Green Plant" that man must not be smug about his
knowledge of "reality." In some of his earlier verse, Stevens was so intent on
defining the transforming power of the imagination that he did not do justice
to the "real," although he insisted again and again that "The real is only the
base. But it is the base" (OP, 160). When he came to write The Rock, he had
become aware of this discrepancy between theory and practice, and "Madame
La Fleurie" (CP, 507) can be read as a kind of symbolic farewell to the poet's
former self. The persona of this poem is punished for his hubris; his knowledge
is "crisp" because "He looked in a glass of the earth and thought he lived in
it." This line may be read in either of two ways: 1) the speaker thought that
he could see through the objects of the external world, or 2) the speaker lived
in a world of mirrors, of reflections once removed from reality. In either case,
his punishment is that there are no bluejays for him to remember now that
he is dead, and Mother Earth becomes for him a "bearded queen, wicked in
her dead light," rather than a "Madame La Fleurie."

"Two Illustrations That the World Is What You Make of It" (CP, 513) is
another interesting cycle poem. It is divided into two parts: the first, "The
Constant Disquisition of the Wind," presents the winter vision, and the
second, "The World Is Larger in Summer," the sunny summer vision. The
dichotomy, however, is not at all sharp. Part I begins on a note of gloom:

> The sky seemed so small that winter day,
> A dirty light on a lifeless world,
> Contracted like a withered stick.

The key word here is "seemed." As the poem progresses, the seemingly hostile wind stirs the speaker's imagination, and he is able to overcome, at least partially, the mood of barrenness and emptiness, and to become creative:

> The appropriate image of himself
> So formed, became himself and he breathed
> The breath of another nature as his own.

The creative vision is only "momentary," but it does occur, and so "Sunday's" "idleness" becomes, ironically, "violent idleness."

In Part II we have the reverse. The artist's imagination flourishes in the summer world: "He discovered the colors of the moon / In a single spruce, when suddenly, / The tree stood dazzling in the air," and, finally, "The master of the spruce, himself, / Became transformed." But this vision does not last either; in the end there are "only the fragments found in the grass / From his project as finally magnified." The world, then, is not really much "larger" in summer, and, as the title of the poem tells us, "the world is what you make of it." Despite all appearances, winter may be the proper imaginative context and summer, to use Eliot's phrase, "the dry season."

The "turning instant of the now" is the subject of another cycle poem in *The Rock*, "Long And Sluggish Lines" (*CP*, 522). It begins as follows:

> It makes so little difference, at so much more
> Than seventy, where one looks, one has been there before.

The winter vision is conveyed in the three following couplets, of which only the first rhymes. The highly irregular cadence of these lines, with their numerous spondees, makes them indeed "long and sluggish." But in the fourth couplet the "opposite" sets in, and what follows is the early spring vision: the "yellow patch" made by sunlight on a wall, the "first fly," the "babyishness of forsythia," and the "makings of the nude magnolia"—all these are humorously described as "these-escent-issant pre-personae," suggesting that which is "incessant," "effervescent," "nascent," and so on. Death is once more "the mother of beauty" (*CP*, 68), and life is renewed. But the last two couplets contain a note of hesitancy unknown to the woman of "Sunday Morning." "Wanderer," the poet-narrator addresses himself,

> this is the pre-history of February.
> The life of the poem in the mind has not yet begun.
> You were not born yet when the trees were crystal
> Nor are you now, in the wakefulness inside a sleep.

The paradox, "wakefulness inside a sleep," implies that the sense of renewal of life, the spring vision, is perhaps only a fantasy. At any rate, Frank Kermode

is not quite accurate when he says of this poem, "despair at repetition
. . . gives way to a certainty of freshness yet to come."

Stevens is much more positive about the renewal of life in another poem
in *The Rock*, "The Hermitage at the Center" (*CP*, 505). Here "death is the
mother of beauty" with a vengeance. The first four tercets each divide into two
parts: the first line defines the winter vision, the harsh reality; the second two
lines present a spring vision, in which "the desired / Reclines in the tempera-
ture of heaven." The fifth tercet then fuses the two:

> And yet this end and this beginning are one,
> And one last look at the ducks is a look
> At lucent children round her in a ring.

We are told here that death and life meet to form a circle which is eternity,
but I do not think that the first four tercets have prepared us for this insight.
It is, for one thing, almost impossible to read the lines in sequence because
the break after each opening line is too abrupt. What we must do is to read
the four opening lines as one unit and the four couplets as a second unit.
Despite the dash after each opening line and the repeated indentation of lines
two and three, the poem seems to split apart into two poems; there is no fusion
in the first four tercets, and so it is difficult to believe in the assertion of fusion
in the fifth tercet. The hermitage "at the Center" seems, in fact, to be perilously
close to the edge: there is a split vision rather than a double vision here.

What is to my mind the most beautiful cycle poem in *The Rock* is the final
poem, "Not Ideas about the Thing but the Thing Itself" (*CP*, 534).[15] Again,
the moment presented is the mysterious turning point from winter to spring,
from death to life. The "bird's cry" which comes from "outside" at "the earliest
ending of winter," arouses the aged speaker from "the vast ventriloquism /
Of sleep's faded papier-mâché." The bird, "A chorister whose c preceded the
choir," heralds the return of the sun which "was rising at six / No longer a
battered panache above snow. . . . " And the knowledge that the life-giving
sun is about to return is "like / A new knowledge of reality."

It is a moment of insight, of great splendor, but also one of pain. The bird's
cry is twice referred to as "scrawny," and the speaker has to tell himself three
times that the sun is coming from "outside," as if he wants to convince himself
that it really *is* outside and not "a sound in his mind." In the end, the "colossal
sun" is "Still far away." The renewal of life is sensed intuitively, but the
awareness of continuity is muted and hesitant; the short, choppy lines as well
as the repeated use of the "It was . . . " construction emphasize this quality.
The title of the poem is particularly ironic because the poem, it turns out,
presents, not the "thing itself " at all, but a very individual "idea about the
thing"—one man's sense of the world.

---

15. For an earlier, less satisfactory treatment of a similar theme, see "The Brave Man" (CP, 138).

"Not Ideas about the Thing but the Thing Itself" may be glossed by a stanza from the famous "To an Old Philosopher in Rome" (*CP*, 508), in which the seasonal metaphor is discarded, so that we are left with the life-death antinomy in its starkest form:

> It is a kind of total grandeur at the end,
> With every visible thing enlarged and yet
> No more than a bed, a chair and moving nuns,
> The immensest theatre, the pillared porch,
> The book and candle in your ambered room. . . .

Riddel, in an otherwise excellent discussion of "To an Old Philosopher," argues that the life of Santayana provides a "most powerful metaphor for Stevens' belief in the redemptive powers of the secular imagination." This is, it seems to me, to overstate the case, for the poem abounds in oxymoron and paradox: i.e., "Unintelligible absolution," "master and commiserable man," "Your dozing in the depths of wakefulness," "afflatus of ruin." In the last stanza, the crucial words "As if" are often overlooked: does the "design of all his [Santayana's] words" really "take form"? There is no "total grandeur" "at the end," only "a kind of total grandeur," a "kind of solemnity" ("An Old Man Asleep"), or "the stale grandeur of annihilation" ("Lebensweisheitspielerei"). The "Rock" of the title poem, "the gray particular of man's life" can be "covered" and "cured" by "leaves," but it is above all,

> The stone from which he rises, up—and—ho,
> The step to the bleaker depths of his descents. . . .

In discussing Stevens's ironic mode, I have hoped to direct attention to the poems as poems, rather than to the poems as philosophical arguments, as most critics would have it. If we insist on tracing Transcendentalist, Platonist, or Bergsonian themes in *The Rock,* we are likely to be disappointed and to find, as do Pearce and Fraser, that the late poems lack "tension" or "humanity" or "particularization." If, on the other hand, we take the poems at face value and read them quite literally, we shall find a very artful "reconciliation of opposites." In *The Rock,* reality and imagination are at last the coequals Stevens had always wished them to be.

Denis Donohue has suggested that the poet's evolution from *Harmonium* to *The Rock* is very much like Yeats's evolution from *The Green Helmet* to *The Wild Swans at Coole.* The point is very well taken: one need only compare, say, "A High-Toned Old Christian Woman" (*Harmonium*) to "St. Armorer's Church From The Outside" (*The Rock*), both poems that ostensibly reject orthodox religion, to note the difference. In the early poem, there is a slightly unpleasant note of bravado; the speaker seems to take excessive delight in debunking the old woman with her narrow religious views. In "St. Armorer's," the boastful tone is no longer present. The speaker's private "chapel" is won

only by means of severe mental strain. This personal chapel, which is to replace
St. Armorer's, the symbol of orthodoxy, rises from "Terre Ensevelie,"

> An ember yes among its cindery noes
> His own: a chapel of breath, an appearance made
> For a sign of meaning in the meaningless. . . .

The chapel, symbolic of Stevens' private religious faith, is further defined as
"A sacred syllable rising from sacked speech. . . . " This line sums up the central
ironic tension, not only of this poem but of *The Rock* as a whole: the "sacred
syllable" and the "sacked speech"—the two must, finally, coexist.

From *American Literature,* 36 (1964), 327-42.

FRANK DOGGETT

Stevens' Later Poetry

I

A GIFT for the irrelevant is the special genius of the past half century in writing. James, Yeats, Joyce, Eliot and Stevens, for instance, each in his own way uses material offered by the inapposite activity of the mind. By its engagement of irrelevance in the purposes of form, literature represents the concern of our age to impose by will an order on the appalling and countless litter of existence. For the great talents the irrelevant is not the isolated, the single instance without connection. For them any irrelevancy is "any stick of the mass / Of which we are too distantly a part." And by the achievement of style they avoid the stigma of the arbitrary.

Resemblance is the quality that seems for Stevens to gather the sticks into a keeping even so modest in its assimilation as the mass. Analogy in Stevens is not only the foundation of metaphor, but the very structure that underlies his individual style. There is hardly a sentence in Stevens' last three books without appositives, appositive substantives or phrases; and the predicate nominative, a related form of thought, becomes increasingly frequent in the later poems. Although these forms of expression appear as statements of equivalence, they are really listings of analogies. "Poetry is almost incredibly one of the effects of analogy," Stevens says, and explains that resemblances are the bases of a poet's style, of the details of his poetry, of things inseparable from style, as context always is, like the organization of his ideas, his quality of tone, his sense of the world, of destiny even. The likenesses of things or, perhaps, the resemblances among the concepts of them in the mind, are trails that Stevens follows in his long search for reality.

Mastery of the irrelevant by Stevens is especially a rhetorical achievement. In his case the beginnings of a style are hidden between the undergraduate pieces and the maturity of *Harmonium*. There suddenly it is, and it seems enough for some critics that it remain that way. But poetry must change, Stevens explicitly states, as well as be abstract and give pleasure. A change, for poetry, is a change in style. The subjects tend to remain the same. Stevens' changes are satisfactorily organic and accordant, from "Sunday Morning" to "An Ordinary Evening in New Haven."

The later style of an old poet is never quite a new one. Poets whose creative period extends into old age cast features of their early success into the mould of a personal convention; they evolve some form of specialization of the early manner. Wallace Stevens developed a later style by a chastening and a reduction. He focussed his genius into the aphoristic range that had always been a part of his earlier work. In *The Auroras of Autumn* and *The Rock* the imagery is more spare, the mere assertions more frequent, the flamboyant lyricism is subdued; the anecdotal approach to idea becomes an expository one.

Stevens' long meditation on the nature of experience, "An Ordinary Evening in New Haven," is the most typical poem of the later style, as "Page from a Tale" is possibly its most atypical. Tendencies of the later style characterize "Notes Toward a Supreme Fiction," or even as early a poem as "The Man with the Blue Guitar," and emerge fully developed in "Description Without Place." Although the later style is a development of elements that go counter to so much that is justly admired in *Harmonium,* it is contended here that it is a great style, and that in it Stevens wrote poems that contribute to the triumphs of language in our day. The rhetorical successes of *Harmonium* obscure the achievement of *The Auroras of Autumn* only when the repetition of those successes is desired or expected.

Poems of the later period have the appearance of gleanings from a commonplace and are written with a reiteration of schemes and topics that gives them the advantages of platitude, its authority and acceptance and recognition, but platitude that is individual, personal, and without the drawbacks of common triteness, blunted, exhausted, fitted to everyone and therefore to no one. Stevens is "he that of repetition is most master." In the later books he uses variations on a few arrangements of thought; his sentence forms are recurrent, his devices of imagery and symbol are open and familiar.

To a large degree it is the virtuosity of tone of the later books that gives Stevens the appearance of having a luxuriant, exotic style. The rapid shifts in attitude, familiar to us from the first pages of *Harmonium,* are characteristic of the later poems, too. But the tone is deepened and the lyrics of *The Auroras of Autumn* and *The Rock,* in spite of their ironic lightness and twistings and turnings of unexpected feeling, are tragic meditations. These books elude the accepted lyric attitudes in surprises and inventions of tone.

The tyranny of style of an age can be seen in the general conformity to the accepted tone of that age, like that to the dominant attitudes and feelings of the past century, its "romantic intoning," its uniform and sometimes monotonous attitude of serious importance. Stevens' play with attitude as well as with language first brought against him the charge of dandyism. All poets play with language; only the truly original with anything else. The tantalizingly exact but unusual sense of his words, the apparently foolish that turns into the poignant or the essential, and the real that is like an aspect of the pointless, are some of the ways in which he expresses his tonal ingenuity. Stevens, in characterizing reality, also describes his lyric strategy:

> The color is almost the color of comedy,
> Not quite. It comes to the point and at the point,
> It fails. The strength at the centre is serious.

> Perhaps instead of failing it rejects
> As a serious strength rejects pin-idleness.

and he concludes:

> The serious reflection is composed
> Neither of comic nor tragic but of commonplace.

With that last word he indicates the importance of platitude as well as that of common experience in its most immediate forms, its frequent, accessible, unnoticed aspect; the gurgling of the water spout, the "baker and butcher blowing," "the tin plate, the loaf of bread on it, / The long-bladed knife, the little to drink and her / Misericordia." As in his new fashion in titles and in some cases their meaning ("An Ordinary Evening in New Haven," "The Plain Sense of Things"), he shows in his later books the uses for poetry of the usual, but never in the way that the conventional realist does, with his realism the other side of the coin of sentimentality.

Beneath its opacity Stevens' late style is characteristically natural, candid, almost ingenuous. The reference of a Stevens' symbol is little more than a stress on its conventional connotations—for example, his representation of the human intelligence by the owl in "Woman Looking at a Vase of Flowers." In general, the poet's theme here is the transformation of the abstract into the actual, a concentration of space and time and sun into a vase of flowers:

> The crude and jealous formlessness
> Became the form and the fragrance of things
> Without clairvoyance, close to her.

The poem is suffused in light and color and the poet expresses his realization that this concept of brightness exists in a mind encased in the absolute darkness of the body, a realization conveyed merely by the symbol of the owl and its associated meaning as the creature who sees in darkness:

> Hoot, little owl within her, how
> High blue became particular
> In the leaf and bud.

With their reference the conventional figurative extension of an image, his symbols are often recurrent abbreviated metaphors; the rock for the certainties of existence, light for awareness, for a consciousness, simple cold for inanimate external reality, fire for the "celestial possible," weather for the felt character of experience as environment, autumn for age. The color symbols, too, turn connotative into primary meanings, making blue the sense of something imagined or conceived, red the sense of something real or observed, black the primal ground of being, green the affective with the life-fulfillment suggestiveness of summer. Of course, these are not set arrangements always seen through

the symbols' transparency; they are given here to show some specific uses of
the reference. A context always brings out special elements in the reference of
a symbol.

Imagery in the later poems tends to be slight, and often only partly emer-
gent. Nearly all is used to present concept rather than to perform the usual
descriptive or decorative or particularizing functions of imagery. Even when
more elaborate and decorative, they are expressive of idea as in the case of the
beautiful image of "Things of August III" (like an early Chirico) that is part
of the metaphor that presents the poet who believes in his simple apprehension
of the objects of the external world:

> Which, being green and blue, appease him,
> By chance, or happy chance, or happiness,
> According to his thought, in the Mediterranean
> Of the quiet of the middle of the night,
> With the broken statues standing on the shore.

The interior character of experience is indicated by the word Mediterranean,
meaning middle earth—within the body. The middle of the night emphasizes
the fact that perception exists within the darkness of the body. Away on the
shore, memories crumble, the broken statues that are the ruins of what was
at one time immediate experience and hence once intact, complete like the once
perfect antique world.

In all of his work an almost naive employment of personification is an aspect
of his use of imagery to present idea, like his giants that personify generaliza-
tions. Entire poems ("Chocorua to Its Neighbor," "The Owl in the Sarcopha-
gus," for instance) are elaborations of this old, familiar device. Poem XXV of
"An Ordinary Evening in New Haven" personifies the conception that each
forms of himself by accretions of experience and judgments ("a hatching that
stared and demanded an answering look"). This poem that expresses one's
consciousness of self includes in its presentation of a sense of separateness some
feeling of evaluation being made in terms of an external condition, a projection
of our own viewing and conception and judging of self in the person of the
hidalgo. We are always conscious that we are alive and the hidalgo (with his
guitar suggesting feeling or the texture of experience) seems slightly inappro-
priate in view of the opening lines, and a sense of one's inappropriateness in
the context of existence is part of this objectification of self.

> Life fixed him, wandering on the stair of glass,
> With its attentive eyes. And, as he stood,
> On his balcony, outsensing distances,
>
> There were looks that caught him out of empty air.
> *C'est toujours la vie qui me regarde* . . . This was
> Who watched him, always, for unfaithful thought.

This sat beside his bed, with its guitar,
To keep him from forgetting, without a word,
A note or two disclosing who it was.

Nothing about him ever stayed the same,
Except this hidalgo and his eye and tune,
The shawl across one shoulder and the hat.

The use of imagery to represent idea is typical here in the reference of the stairs to existence, the balcony to present point of view, outsensing distances to remembering or imagining beyond the immediate. Actually a whole field of reflection and feeling is represented with the instances given above mere aspects. The essential ideas of the late poems are abstractions for which an interpretation becomes a pinning down of one or another feasibility, a "possible for its possibleness."

The essential idea of "What We See is What We Think" concerns a point of change, and if we particularize the change in some way (as an intimation of night or mortality or aging, or as the influence of preconcept on perception) this would be a part of the character of one experience of reading it. "An Ordinary Evening in New Haven XXIV" is another poem that is expressive of the same abstraction, the point of change, although the experiences this poem conveys are as different from the other as the possibilities of particularizing its central abstraction, considering the suggestion of a "Second Coming" and the wit of its allusion to Boethius in the first line: "The consolations of space are nameless things." Boethius, we can remember, names the consolations of philosophy in elaborate personifications, and Stevens, after his opening statement of the emptiness of belief in our day, names one consolation to be a personification of "Incomincia," a beginning of something new, of a new age.

It was after the neurosis of winter. It was
In the genius of summer that they blew up

The statue of Jove among the boomy clouds.
It took all day to quieten the sky
And then to refill its emptiness again,

So that at the edge of afternoon, not over,
Before the thought of evening had occurred
Or the sound of Incomincia had been set,

There was a clearing, a readiness for first bells,
An opening for outpouring, the hand was raised.

At any rate, these poems are lyric meditations that allow various deductions for those who want deductions. Of course, the important thing for each poem is not a pinning down, a restrictive interpretation, but the thing that it is, the character of one's experience with it, its whole texture of meaning.

II

Lately it is hard to say when metaphor begins and bare assertion ends (as in this sentence itself). The more we look, it seems, the more we find that is metaphorical. Since its formation is so mysterious, its nature so pervasive, perhaps we are right to discuss mostly the effects of metaphor, its transformation of the spirit. Intent as we have been on the nature of experience in the last few centuries, our interest in the psychology of metaphor was natural and characteristic. Metaphor as a distinctive element in experience was in back of Coleridge's discussion of imagination. Even the semantic studies of more recent years illustrate the prevailing interest of the age, for the analysis of meaning is an analysis of what happens to the mind.

When we try to describe its structure, the idea of metaphor dropped into the mind makes ever-widening circles of inclusion, a characteristic of most concepts that disturb us into attempts to enclose by definition. Of course, it's the interaction of two or more obvious images, merged in aspect and yet separate in essence, that provides the metaphor of traditional discussion. A closer look may disclose that non-metaphoric poetry or even non-metaphoric speech is impossible. Within the language itself is a residual life that comes from its origin in the activity of the animate creature. Language cannot be separated from function in living, from movement, feeling, interpretation of perception, from circumstance. In circumstance especially, metaphor emerges; for language creates and refers to a certain existence, an existence of the thing expressed by language, apart from the continuous narrative we sense in our own life, our own circumstance, and conveys meaning with a continuous hidden imagery that is analogous to the continuous life of sensation and activity of the living being. It is a reference from one occurrence to another, from the self to this thing, this meaning that the self has created, and by the conjunction of the life of the mind and the life of the self in perception of externals, language in its very existence is metaphorical. One could mention grammatical and rhetorical structure as based on an imagery drawn from the life of action, or could remark that even our simplest word order, subject-verb-object, implies an image of an activity, and this image of action, carried from subject to object, is metaphorical.

Some quite ordinary forms of expression provide effects that resemble those of usually recognized metaphor. Relationships and conjunctions of concepts are provided by the device of apposition and of predicate nominative. For predicate nominative we can quote Stevens' "seeming is description without place" to recall that the predicate is related to the subject like a statement of the equality and identity of one thing and another. Apposition gives much the same kind of sense of equalization of two things, except that the commas substitute for the verb to be:

Jerome and the scrupulous Francis and Sunday women,
The nurses of the spirit's innocence.

These two devices say that one image, one concept, one substantive, is equal
to another, although by the very statement of equivalence, or by the appositive
position, it is implied that the equality is really an identity of aspects and a
separation of essences, like the relationships in metaphor. In its simple forms
conventional metaphor has the shape of the predicate nominative.

The green roses drifted up from the table
In smoke

is a metaphoric statement of Stevens' that roses equal smoke in this particular
experience. Of course, there are more implications than this, but the example
is sufficient to show the structural resemblance of the two forms.

These assertions of resemblance which appear to be statements of equalization, or these series of modifications which seem to be reconsiderations, the
predicate nominative which says this is that, or the appositive which states that
one thing becomes another, another, another—these are the characteristic
forms of Wallace Stevens' later style, especially of *The Auroras of Autumn*. The
frequent recurrence of these forms gives the later poems their special air of
abstraction, their appearance of lyric philosophy. Our sense of style is our sense
of repetition within rhetoric.

The statement of equivalence gives to poetry some of the effect of the axiom,
its accepted verity and essential rightness. It is an indigenous feature of American writing and thinking and, in part, no doubt, a burgeoning from the
moralizing strain in colonial literature with its reliance on the Bible and the
popular maxim. Poor Richard and the Psalmist speak through the sententious
assertions of Thoreau and Emerson and Holmes, in the didacticism of the last
century. Most of the poems of Emily Dickinson use the sentence form of the
definition and the air of aphorism. In our own day the great lyric aphorists are
Frost and Stevens.

Of course, the aphoristic tendency shows up early in Stevens, in "Man is
the intelligence of his soil" and its vice-versa, "The Comedian as the Letter
C," for instance, but not so often as to be the dominant mode of expression
that it is in *The Auroras of Autumn* and *The Rock*. The special quality of the
late style is so permeated with the effects of apposition that some criticism has
felt that it resembles improvisation. That effect is given because in apposition
the poet seems to deliberate about his original concept. He appears to reconsid-
er it by seeking an equivalent in another and another version, continuously
altered yet presented as though it were the same. Also, predicate nominative
has the air of an attempt at definition, as though in explanation.

"The rock is the gray particular of man's life," "The house is evening,
half dissolved," "The poem is the cry of its occasion," "The town was a
residuum, / A neuter shedding shapes in an absolute," "The poet is / The
angry day-son clanging at its make: / The satisfaction underneath the sense,

/ The conception sparkling in still obstinate thought"—these are not only characteristic forms of the late poetry, but of the prose. As they express resemblances almost to the point of identification, these grammatical forms are part of the inner structure of Stevens' sense of reality. "Poetry is a satisfying of the desire for resemblance," Stevens says, and feels that by resemblance poetry "touches the sense of reality, it enhances the sense of reality, heightens it, intensifies it."

The two forms of his style, which offer resemblances through assertions of equivalence, can be called verbal equations—to borrow a useful term from Empson. All sorts of conjunctions provide some of the effects of conventional metaphor but the effects of verbal equations are borne by balances of meaning. There can be no merging of aspects until the possibilities in common meaning between the two concepts are understood, as in these subtle balances of idea: "Description is revelation," "The eye's plain version is a thing apart," "words of the world are the life of the world." Looking into the nature of Stevens' verbal equations, we find them to be a certain kind of realization. A realization of this nature is sudden insight into relationship, and as such can be taken to be a metaphor of the abstract as in this verbal equation of poetry and the life of the mind:

> . . . the theory
> Of poetry is the theory of life,
>
> As it is, in the intricate evasions of as,
> In things seen and unseen, created from nothingness,
> The heavens, the hells, the worlds, the longed-for lands.

The realization here is of the interrelationships of the nature of poetry and of experience. Their use of metaphor "in the intricate evasions of as" is their way of touching reality, of avoiding yet meeting unapproachable blank fact by seeking resemblances, and understanding one thing in terms of another. These interrelationships extend to reverberations of meaning in poetry and interpretation in experience ("things seen and unseen"), to the inventions of poetry and the self, to their conceived aversions, their longed-for conceptions, their definitions of feeling through idea. In this respect "the point of vision and desire are the same."

The lyric strategy of Stevens' later style based in the nature of realization—of identifications, of illumination provided by the recognition of conjunction of ideas, with modifications offered by other successive concepts presented appositively—reminds us of the poet's expressed interest in the plastic arts. The later poems have a static quality, as of things or ideas placed in relation to each other, like arrangements of meaning. Speaking of "The Relations Between Poetry and Painting," Stevens said: "The counterpart of Villon in poetry, writing as he paints, would concern himself with like things (but not necessarily confining himself to them), creating the same sense of aesthetic certainty, the same sense of exquisite realization and the same sense of being modern and living." The poems of *Harmonium* are essentially dramatic, with the emphasis on a certain situation with the involvement of person and the dominance of the verb and descriptive words and images (for the descriptive belongs more to the narrative than to the plastic, the static). Repetitions, resemblances, recognitions, ideas with their influences and modifications one upon another, their "radial aspects," the dominance of nouns and the continuous connective sense of the verb "to be" in recurring patterns of relationship create a condition in which the mind moves upon these areas of contemplation as on the related forms and suggestiveness within a painting. This is an analogy that should be carried no farther but does have at least the value of pointing to inner qualities of Stevens' late style.

III

There is always within a poem a dual vision, a sense of the world within the poem and a sense of the poet's own world beyond the poem. The poem itself presents a voice and its occasion. This is the world of the poem. Then a special world of the human lot emanates from the judgments and references to externals, and from the particular concerns of the poet, his considerations of belief and his concept of life and value, and our temporary consideration, too, as we enter the experience of the poem. This is a world shared with the poet through the medium of his poetry as well as his opinions from other writings. Like the foreground in old pictures, we are aware of both worlds at once, and sometimes they are complementary and again the relationship is merely referential. There are, plainly enough, other courses of events while reading, like that of the historical conditions of the poet, or of one's own personal view of things. The moment of cognizance within a poem is always the center of an infinite series of concentric circumstances. For convenience, the world within the poem will be referred to as the poem's circumstance, and the idea of a world implied by the opinions and concepts that give a view of man will be called the poet's sense of the world, to use a phrase of Stevens. No ordered, philosophic system is implied by the poet's sense of the world, merely the environment of human conditions and the basic concepts that give structure to a sense of eventualities. "Poetry does not address itself to beliefs," Stevens asserts, perhaps by implication chiding those critics who must always look for doctrine and consequently always find it.

If beliefs are never the objects of his poetry, neither are they its subjects. "What is the poet's subject? It is his sense of the world," Stevens says in "Effects of Analogy" and goes on to refer indirectly to the importance of his sense of the world to his own poetry. In general his subjects are nearly always, in *The Auroras of Autumn* and *The Rock,* some aspect of the transformation of external reality into experience, of "form gulping after formlessness"; or when they are not, the contrary theme, formlessness gulping after form, the traditional concern with death and delapidation, is often dominant.

The poet's sense of the world gives a perspective and background to the circumstances of his poems with the special sense of destiny that characterizes and intensifies their quality of feeling. To suggest formal belief is a risk that has to be taken in presenting Stevens' sense of the world, but the risk vanishes

if the suggestion of belief is relegated to mere inference when a reader turns
to the poems.

Like the early poems, the later ones give the human as, of necessity, the
center of his universe, and a universe largely inanimate, unfriendly, unhostile,
unknowably vast and intricate outside the small, intense self. We still have the
eye of the blackbird among twenty snowy mountains. The concept of tragedy
of the later poems is that of the human with its warm feeling, its affections,
gaiety and tenderness of the title poem of *The Auroras of Autumn,* with its inner
gentleness and wish for some brave relation with external matter before the
meaningless fact of extinction, like the terrible irony of "Page from a Tale,"
of the man alone on the arctic ice, by his small fire, with his bits of memory
of Yeats' "The Lake Isle of Innisfree." Necessity, "the will of wills," necessity
in having to live in and in having to die, is the framing of Stevens' view of
destiny. Within the frame is festival, and charity, and vitality, and lightning
cognition, and musing. The mind's luminosity has taken the ancient place of
the indestructible spirit and is extinguishable like the light-image that Stevens
uses to symbolize the living consciousness.

> The scholar of one candle sees
> An Arctic effulgence flaring on the frame
> Of everything he is. And he feels afraid.

Stevens continues in the final books to present the tragic in the idea of man
more sure of emptiness and space than of divinity and transcendental love, but
in a new vein he expresses a yearning for some innocence to be an actuality
central to all being, even though he never admits more belief in it than the
mere presence of concept.

> That it should be, and yet not be, a thing
>
> That pinches the pity of the pitiful man,
> Like a book at evening beautiful but untrue,
> Like a book on rising beautiful and true.

In his evening, autumn, old age, Stevens continually regards death, continually seeing mere extinction there, with any other belief no more than the
consolation that man seeks in turning away from the bare fact of mortality.

> It is a child that sings itself to sleep,
> The mind, among the creatures that it makes.

The world that Stevens conceives is not a mechanistic world simplified into
a succession of images and events, and reduced to the surface of reality as
though we knew it all in immediate perception of forms. The physical, infinite
in change and conceptual possibility, is itself transcendant.

> As if the air, the mid-day air was swarming
> With the metaphysical changes that occur,
> Merely in living as and where we live.

Stevens does not include in his sense of the world any ardency of belief; and to find strong evaluation or judgment is misinterpretation like that of looking for racial prejudice in his colloquial use of racial terms. His is poetry of another, perhaps a purer kind, and finds its intensity in a passion for the straight look at that which is forever varying, uncertain, the nature of experience and its basis in reality. This is his constant meditation in the later poems on the central mystery of experience, the turning instant of the now, that moment when the meaningless becomes awareness, when attention selects and interprets external chaos, the self creating its reality in its own likeness. It is the theme of two of Stevens' greatest passages: "Be thou me" from "Notes Toward a Supreme Fiction" and the opening section of the title poem of *The Auroras of Autumn*. The poems of this book, as of *The Rock* or *Transport to Summer*, resume over and over the search for reality.

> . . . the philosopher's search
>
> For an interior made exterior
> And the poet's search for the same exterior made
> Interior. . . .

It is the ambiguous character of experience, its internal-external ambivalence, that forms the major part of Stevens' later sense of the world, like the environment of objects that we *seem* to see without and about us, but that he realizes as an image floating at head level and enclosed and individual, the reality within each mind:

> Not that which is but that which is apprehended,
> A mirror, a lake of reflections in a room,
> A glassy ocean lying at the door,
>
> A great town hanging pendant in a shade.

The later poems do not present imagination and reality as in opposition but include in the particulars of reality the imagined and the perceived as both imagined *and* perceived, both of these as forms of conception.

> We seek
> Nothing beyond reality. Within it,
>
> Everything, the spirit's alchemicana
> Included, the spirit that goes roundabout
> And through included, not merely the visible,

> The solid, but the movable, the moment,
> The coming on of feasts and the habits of saints,
> The pattern of the heavens and high, night air.

Yet there is the self apart and the actual presence of externals to be reckoned with; and between the two, mysterious as their juncture in the mind, is the unknowable division, the breach between being as living experience and the object detached yet imminent in its presence. Analogies are the only bridge over this gap between presence and concept.

> They help us face the dumbfoundering abyss
> Between us and the object, external cause,
> The little ignorance that is everything.

Analogy itself Stevens regards as an aspect of reality, and is fascinated by resemblances between the human and inanimate as in the early days of the roaring wind seeking its syllable. His sense of analogy ranges from mere semblance "like a meaning in nothingness" to metaphoric analogy like that of his image for creativity, for the human imagination with its repetitiousness and numberless small variations, "The branches sweeping in the rain," of "An Ordinary Evening in New Haven."

Resemblances are the connections sought after by the mind in composing to itself the particulars of reality. But these particulars impose their own nature on each other, on the mind too, creating contingency by mere presence and contiguity like the action of a sort of residual will. Such relationships involve an effect of the seeming of one thing upon the seeming of another, and thus transform analogy into influence. In some poems ("An Ordinary Evening in New Haven XIX" or "XXIX") he suggests that each thing has its "radial aspect," its effect on the related or the contiguous, and helps create the assembled nature of integers. This effect forms and colors and characterizes concept until experience becomes a shadow whose form is the pattern that influence casts from external reality. In this sense, "The world images for the beholder," even though, as in "Holiday in Reality," all experience is individual and the external world must be an extension of oneself. In fact, the pathetic fallacy may have pathetic aspects but is hardly a fallacy as indicated in "What We See Is What We Think."

Stevens makes his most elaborate statement of the search for reality in "An Ordinary Evening in New Haven." Like most of his long poems, it is a segmented, discontinuous meditation. In the opening sections the idea of reality as an external gives way to that of the reality within the self, the fresh living moment of existence, and he conceives the flow of awareness as a perpetual reference of the reality within to that without. The nature of fact or object, its multiple possibility as it enters the now of the self, and the elaborations and interpretations of the mind are some of the considerations of reality in early sections of the poem.

A topical discussion of this poem would commit its exposition to the error of considering Stevens as an advocate of an epistemological theory. The late manner does resemble that of philosophical statement; we can almost expect logical forms; we look for a consistent organization of thought; it seems that a paraphrase is almost possible, that we can state a certain meaning for a certain poem, an effort that misses most of its purpose, like telling dreams or describing music. Stevens, in spite of appearance, is never a philosophical poet except (like other poets) in his interest in the theory of reality. One can answer some attempts to distill a system of ideas from his poetry by another divergent distillation. His ideas are not systemic but thematic. What seems a development of doctrine is a version of experience.

"Thus poetry becomes," Stevens says, "and is a transcendent analogue composed of the particulars of reality, created by the poet's sense of the world, that is to say, his attitude, as he intervenes and interposes the appearances of that sense."

For Stevens, the particulars of reality include the interposition of his sense of the world. The effort to express reality is part of that reality that he wishes to express. In the last section (XXXI) of "An Ordinary Evening in New Haven" he indicates the cumulative, mutant nature of reality, its activity in experience and, at the same time, the accretion of its particulars as meaning, through the poet's rhetoric. There he conceives reality as not only the processes of the instant in progress and formative coalescence, but the things that never quite happen, the beginnings and abandonments, the poisings and turnings. Writing a poem is an instance, even language itself with its ignored occurrences and its possibilities and conjurations. Section XXXI implies such a sense of the world and by its interrupted movement and succession of appositives suggests its own statements of "the edgings and inchings of final form." Even the puns possible in reds and drum, the light-life symbolism, the ironic finikins and fidgets of human value are swarming activities themselves of statement.

The three instances of the basic miracles of meaning: symbolism, metaphor, synechdoche, are placed appropriately in the stanza before that last one in which he projects reality in what is almost, but not quite, an image:

> The less legible meanings of sounds, the little reds
> Not often realized, the lighter words
> In the heavy drum of speech, the inner men
>
> Behind the outer shields, the sheets of music
> In the strokes of thunder, dead candles at the window
> When day comes, fire-foams in the motions of the sea,
>
> Flickings from finikin to fine finikin
> And the general fidget from busts of Constantine
> To photographs of the late president, Mr. Blank,
>
> These are the edgings and inchings of final form,
> The swarming activities of the formulae

Of statement, directly and indirectly getting at,

Like an evening evoking the spectrum of violet,
A philosopher practicing scales on his piano,
A woman writing a note and tearing it up.

It is not in the premise that reality
Is a solid. It may be a shade that traverses
A dust, a force that traverses a shade.

In fortunate passages like this Stevens expresses his genius for realization through a kind of rhetorical shorthand, and instead of the expected development of the usual idea, adjusts the movements of thought, the changes of tone, to the exigencies of the mastery of irrelevance for that particular occasion. Our own realization of that genius will take time and meanwhile the poetry, for those who read it, will accomplish the changes in sensibility that can lead to its subtle disclosures.

From *ELH: A Journal of English Literary History*, 25 (1958), 137-54. Revised 1971 by the author.

SELECTED BIBLIOGRAPHY

Works

The Necessary Angel: Essays on Reality and the Imagination. New York: Alfred A. Knopf, 1951.
The Collected Poems of Wallace Stevens. New York: Alfred A. Knopf, 1954.
Opus Posthumous. New York: Alfred A. Knopf, 1957.

Letters

Letters of Wallace Stevens. Ed. Holly Stevens, New York: Alfred A. Knopf, 1966.

Selections

Poems by Wallace Stevens. Ed. Samuel French Morse. New York: Vintage Books, 1959.
The Palm at the End of the Mind: Selected Poems and a Play. Ed. Holly Stevens. New York: Alfred A. Knopf, 1971.

Bibliography

Morse, Samuel French. *Wallace Stevens: A Preliminary Checklist of His Published Writings: 1898-1954.* New Haven: Yale Univ. Library, 1954.
Bryer, Jackson R., and Riddel, Joseph N. "A Checklist of Stevens Criticism," *Twentieth Century Literature,* VIII (October 1962-January 1963), 124-42.
Morse, Samuel French, Bryer, Jackson R., and Riddel, Joseph N. *Wallace Stevens Checklist and Bibliography of Stevens Criticism.* Denver: Alan Swallow, 1963.
Huguelet, Theodore L. *The Merrill Checklist of Wallace Stevens.* Columbus: Charles E. Merrill, 1970.

Biography

Morse, Samuel French. *Wallace Stevens: Poetry as Life.* New York: Pegasus, 1970.

Criticism

Baird, James. *The Dome and the Rock: Structure in the Poetry of Wallace Stevens.* Baltimore: Johns Hopkins Univ. Press, 1968.
Blessing, Richard Allen. *Wallace Stevens' "Whole Harmonium."* Syracuse: Syracuse Univ. Press, 1970.
Borroff, Marie, ed. *Wallace Stevens: A Collection of Critical Essays.* Englewood Cliffs, N.J.: Prentice-Hall, 1963.
Brown, Ashley, and Haller, Robert S., ed. *The Achievement of Wallace Stevens.* Philadelphia: J.B. Lippincott, 1962.
Brown, Merle E. *Wallace Stevens: The Poem as Act.* Detroit: Wayne State Univ. Press, 1970.
Burney, William A. *Wallace Stevens.* New York: Twayne, 1968.

Buttel, Robert. *Wallace Stevens: The Making of Harmonium.* Princeton: Princeton Univ. Press, 1967.

Doggett, Frank. *Stevens' Poetry of Thought.* Baltimore: Johns Hopkins Univ. Press, 1966.

Enck, John J. *Wallace Stevens: Images and Judgments.* Carbondale: Southern Illinois Univ. Press, 1964.

Fuchs, Daniel. *The Comic Spirit of Wallace Stevens.* Durham, N.C.: Duke Univ. Press, 1963.

Kermode, Frank. *Wallace Stevens.* New York: Grove, 1960.

Lentricchia, Frank. *The Gaiety of Language: An Essay on the Radical Poetics of W.B. Yeats and Wallace Stevens.* Berkeley: Univ. of California Press, 1968.

Nasser, Eugene P. *Wallace Stevens: An Anatomy of Figuration.* Philadelphia: Univ. of Pennsylvania Press, 1965.

O'Connor, William Van. *The Shaping Spirit: A Study of Wallace Stevens.* Chicago: Henry Regnery, 1950.

Pack, Robert. *Wallace Stevens. An Approach to His Poetry and Thought.* New Brunswick, N.J.: Rutgers Univ. Press, 1958.

Pearce, Roy Harvey, and Miller, J. Hillis, ed. *The Act of the Mind: Essays on the Poetry of Wallace Stevens.* Baltimore: Johns Hopkins Univ. Press, 1965.

Riddel, Joseph N. *The Clairvoyant Eye: The Poetry and Poetics of Wallace Stevens.* Baton Rouge: Louisiana State Univ. Press, 1965.

Stern, Herbert J. *Wallace Stevens: Art of Uncertainty.* Ann Arbor: Univ. of Michigan Press, 1966.

Vendler, Helen H. *On Extended Wings: Wallace Stevens' Longer Poems.* Cambridge, Mass.: Harvard Univ. Press, 1969.

Wells, Henry W. *Introduction to Wallace Stevens.* Bloomington: Indiana Univ. Press, 1964.